FEAST
OR
FAMINE

A Cultural Food Journey of the North West of Ireland

EMMETT McCOURT

GUILDHALL PRESS

Published in November 2013

Guildhall Press
Unit 15, Ráth Mór Business Park
Bligh's Lane, Derry
BT48 0LZ
Ireland
(028) 7136 4413
info@ghpress.com
www.ghpress.com

Emmett McCourt
Irish Food Heritage Project
27 Amelia Court, Derry
BT48 8DW
Ireland
Mob: 077 4990 3652
emmett@feastorfamine.ie
www.feastorfamine.ie

Edited by Garbhan Downey.

Cover image © Chris Neely of ModaFoto: www.chrisneely.co.uk

Images copyright © various contributors (see individual credits).

ISBN: 978 1 906271 77 0

A CIP record for this book is available from the British Library.

Guildhall Press gratefully acknowledges the financial support of the Arts Council of Northern Ireland as a principal funder under its Annual Funding Programme.

Acknowledgements

I would like to extend my sincere thanks to all those individuals and organisations that helped me develop the Irish Food Heritage Project and supported me in the research and writing of this book.

For practical and financial support: Staff, lecturers and students of the North West Regional College and its Hospitality Department: Seamus Murphy, Calum Morrison, Kate Duffy, Karen McLaughlin, Conor McGurgan, Geri Martin and Michael McCarron. Minister Michelle O'Neill and Noel Lavery of DARD. Staff of Guildhall Press. Garbhan Downey for his guidance and expertise. Shona McCarthy, Martin Melarkey and Peter Hutcheon of Culture Company 2013. Tony Monaghan, Mary Blake, Brenda Stevenson and Michael Cooper of Derry City Council. David O'Connell and Beverly Coomber of Arts Council NI. Mark Nagurski of Culture Tech and Digital Derry. James and Ian Doherty of Doherty Meats. Michael Moorehead and Steven Miller of the NI Regional Food Programme. Caoimhin Corrigan and Paul Doherty of ILEX. Judith Brannigan and the NI Food and Drink Show. Gillian Lamrock, Andrew Sides and John Pollock of the Loughs Agency. Michael McKillop of Glens of Antrim Potatoes. Seamas Heaney and Leeann Monk of Old Library Trust. Keith Smyton of Ulster Pork & Bacon and the Ulster Farmers Union. Norman Murray of Invest NI.

For advice and guidance: Staff and community of Serenity House, Moville. Maurice McHenry of NI Potato Festival. Alan Healy of North West Marketing. The organisers of Taste of Donegal Food Festival. Tourism Ireland and NI Tourist Board. Karen Henderson and Aoife Thomas of DVCB. Gerry O'Hara, Eibhlín Ní Dhochartaigh, Anne Marie Gallagher, Jim Hamilton, Marie Doherty of Cultúrlann Uí Chanáin, Comhaltas Doire and Fleadh Cheoil na hEireann. Kieran Fegan and Monreagh Ulster Scots Heritage Centre. The Ulster Scots Agency. Creggan Enterprises and Hive Digital Arts Studio at Ráth Mór. Gerry Quinn, Harry Diamond, committee and directors of the River Faughan Anglers. Catriona Logan of the Celtic Media Festival. Feile Grianan Ailigh Committee. Joanne Lewis of GCVB. Foyle Parents and Friends Association. Albert and Irene Titterington of the Great Game Fairs of Ireland. Des Crofton of NARGC. Patrick Doherty of Doe Famine Village. David Matchett and Peter Gott of Borough Market, London.

For media contributions and coverage: Erin Hutcheon, Ellen Barr and Julieann Campbell, *Derry Journal*. Russell Campbell, *LCN* Magazine. BBC Radio Foyle, Drive 102 FM and BBC Radio Ulster. Joe Mahon, Westway Films. Vinny Cunningham and Billy Gallagher, Northland Broadcast. Libraries NI, Derry Central Library, Shantallow Library and the Bigger-McDonald Collection. National Library of Ireland and the Lawrence Collection. US Library of Congress and the American Stereoscopic Company Collection (via Wikimedia Commons). National Museums NI and the National Gallery of Ireland. Julie Forbes and Tern TV. Sarah Reddin, Waddle Media. Brian Mitchell and Bernadette Walsh, Heritage & Museum Service. Brian Lacey, *Discover Derry*. Anne Morrison Smyth and Gary Blair of Ballymoney Ullans Centre. Ken Harron, Barnacle Books. Alan Healy, *Derry News*. Paul Pringle, Harry Cook and Keith Mathews, *Country Sports and Country Life* Magazine.

For encouragement and input: Deputy First Minister Martin McGuinness, Michelle Gildernew, Sean Owens, Conrad Gallagher, Noel McMeel, Paul Rankin, Nick Nairn, John and Vincent Grant, Michele Shirlow, Lindsay Lyttle, Sean Beattie, Jim MacLoughlin, Pádraic Óg Gallagher, Mickey McGuinness, Phil Cunningham, Declan Carlin, Conal McFeely, Mark Lusby, Derek Watson, Vincent McKenna, Graham McClements, John and Pat Hume, Martin Reilly, Jim Shannon, Colum Eastwood, Rory Farrell, Cara Dillon, Sam Lakeman, Odhran Mullan, Johnny Murray, Dee McCafferty, Gareth Austin, Tim and Magdalena Eriksen, Maoliosa Boyle, Alister McReynolds, Gary White Deer, Don Mullan, Richard Moore, Albert Sargent, Mark Sargent, Carole Diamond, Bonnie Weir, Judith Johnston McLoughlin, Abigail McElroy, Mary M Drymon, John R Moore, Emma Cowan, Kathy Jensen, Terry Coyle, Robert Lynch, Richard Craig, Janet Devlin, Leona and Richard Kane. Carole McCorkell, Barry R McCain,

Mark Roberts, Mary O'Neill, Donal McCloy, Michael Irving, David Kelly, Gareth Ferry, Frank J Clement Lorford, Margaret Gallagher, Hugh Gallagher, Bronagh Corr-McNicholl, Frankie McMenamin and Kathleen McKinney. Lecturers and staff at SRC Newry and Belfast Metropolitan College.

Special thanks to all the wonderful photographers who captured the essence of Irish food and whose contributions brought to life the Irish Food Heritage Project and *Feast or Famine*.

Shane Smith of *Yes Chef* Magazine for his passion for food, his eye for detail and for the long hours spent in the pursuit of bringing the past to life: www.nimedia.net

Chris Neely of ModaFoto Photography for the wonderful front-cover image: www.chrisneely.co.uk

Sue Spencer Photography for her perfect portrait shots of great characters and images of the very essence of game dishes: www.suespencerphotography.co.uk

Conor Glynn, Danny Lyttle and Jacky du of the North West Regional College who captured food dishes and college life in all its facets: www.nwrc.ac.uk

Lorcan Doherty Photography, one of the great photographers of the North West: www.lorcan.ie

Derek Laverty Photography, Sporting and Country Life, who captures the very heart of life at the Great Game Fairs of Ireland: www.flickr.com/photos/dereklaverty

Gardiner Mitchell Photography, specialist Irish tourism and angling imagery, for the wonderful film and photography of the Lough Foyle native flat oysters and food photography for the Turner Prize 2013: www.gardinermitchell.com – www.youtube.com/watch?v=RXxZzuN5914

Gary McLoughlin for his kind permission to use images from *The Shamrock and Peach* cook book by Judith McLoughlin: www.shamrockandpeach.com

Phil Cunningham and Hugh Gallagher for some beautiful images of Inishowen and the North West.

Stephen Boyle for his colourful images of Derry's local restaurants and eateries and his coverage of the IFHP guided food tour (City of Derry Food Adventure).

Peter McKane for his wonderful photos of the Irish Food Heritage Project cookery demonstrations. Gerry Temple for being a great supporter of the project and for shadowing and snapping the many events of *Feast or Famine*. Marie Moore McGrellis for her wonderful action photos of cookery demonstrations.

If I have omitted anyone who contributed to this publication or wider project please accept my apologies and I thank you here also.

To my father and mother, Denis and Angela, who taught me how to respect and love all things, cultures and creeds. This book would not have been possible without the continued support and patience of my partner Mary. Sincere thanks.

Many thanks to the many Irish Food Heritage Project partners and sponsors.

Contents

For Mary, Georgia, Danaé and Luke

Foreword

With so many cookery books being published nowadays, it is sometimes difficult to distil the real essence of a collection of food recipes that have any substance. Having said that, this book comprehensively embodies a new approach to telling the previously undisclosed story of our relationship with food, both good and bad.

Feast or Famine is an in-depth, current and highly relevant study of our Irish food journey.

I urge you to delve deeply into Emmett's decidedly personal and fully explored gastronomic expedition. This is a captivating story of the trials and tribulations that have made us all what we are as a people today. We have now come full circle, where, as an island, we now influence food production in all its facets – locally, nationally and internationally.

Emmett McCourt tells this story with a passion, tradition and knowledge that surpasses any previous work of this kind.

I am very proud to have known Emmett and his family for over 25 years and fully understand his drive, enthusiasm and ability to tell this wonderful narrative of Ireland's true connections with food.

I have had the pleasure of Emmett as my trusted Executive Sous-Chef (a true cuisinier) in my restaurants and off-site when cooking for some of Ireland's most important political, economic, sporting and society events and in the promotion of all things food from these shores both at home and abroad.

I remember with great fondness the many long nights that Emmett and I spent engaged in culinary conversations and debates that stretched into the wee small hours (and there are very few people that stay with me with regards to gastronomy as well as all things Derry). These memories will stay with me forever. Thanks, Emmett.

Sean Owens

It would be remiss of me not to underline the importance of these nights for our gastronomic rebirth and exploration. I count Emmett as a true lifelong friend and culinary confidant and to say that I am delighted to have been asked to write this foreword to his first publication would be an understatement.

This work embodies the true spirit of all things 'Feast or Famine' (the title alone had me hooked) and I was captivated from the very first draft I read. There was 'a hunger on me' that was impossible to satisfy; the more I read, the more I wanted. And that's from someone who has 'devoured' thousands of cookbooks over a lifetime of love of food. I couldn't set it down and I felt a rollercoaster of emotions as I got immersed in a story that covered it all: wealth – war – famine – death – humour – emigration – tragedy – celebration – laughter – tears – poverty and plenty. And packed with unique recipes recreating the traditional methods and ingredients of decades of Irish cooking, all splendidly illustrated throughout with first-class photography.

Emmett's extensive experience as a celebrated and renowned chef and respected educator at the top of his profession has allowed him to capture an accurate, yet personal and heartfelt, historical account of the food journey of these shores and freely share it with the rest of the world. Emmett has travelled widely and this experience shines through in his understanding, recollection and narration of some of these earlier culinary excursions from the North West of Ireland.

Many times I have admired with great pride the determination and career developments that have made Emmett the chef and author he has now become. I looked on in awe when Emmett returned to France to work under the great Yves Thuries, the Master Pâtissier. Chefs dream of working with the best. Emmett made this a reality to further his career and broaden his knowledge. The wealth of culinary expertise that he then imparted on his return home allowed Emmett to disseminate the recipes and techniques to many chefs in Ireland both young and old. This lead to his eventual love for teaching and coaching cookery and passing on his repertoire of historical, current and relevant recipes to others.

The research required for the completion of this work is considerable and great credit needs to go to Emmett for staying with it. Undoubtedly, it is a vast and complicated sto-ry to divulge. Many would have given up, not Emmett. He 'kept 'er lit'.

Emmett has compiled a fantastic mix of food facts and anecdotes and has uncovered amazing food stories that have remained untold until now. For this we can only be truly thankful, as otherwise these important accounts would have been lost forever.

It is a magnificent achievement by Emmett who has created a unique reference source for everyone interested in Irish food. When we consider that only 150 years ago, crop failure, famine and death where rife in Ireland, this publication graphically demonstrates that we can now take up our rightful place in the cuisines of western Europe. This work, together with Emmett's very successful Irish Food Heritage Project, educational plans and road shows, will, without doubt, underpin our new and confident Irish food identity.

I am absolutely delighted to have contributed in a very small way to this positive reappraisal and detailed documentation of Irish food and its cultural heritage and traditions. Emmett McCourt will now be recognised throughout the hospitality and tourism world both at home and abroad as the specialist in this field and I eagerly await with relish the second helping. 'Please, sir, can I have some more?'

Sean Owens MCGC MIH LCGI
Chef & Entrepreneur
www.seanowens.net

Introduction
A Culinary Odyssey

Food has been my abiding passion throughout my life. My memories all revolve around it – my journeys and adventures have all centred on it.

I remember as a child, my granny taking me to the Model Nursery School in Derry and loving the walk past Windsor Terrace, where we could revel in the smell of fresh buns from Mickey Ennis's bread van. Many years later, when I was training in France, the smell of the *boulangeries* there would always bring me right back to that same street.

I have been fortunate to travel widely as a chef, experiencing other countries' food and culinary heritage. But it has been the people of my own city and its hinterland who in-stilled the passion that exists in me for food and inspired me on my journey.

When I first started cooking professionally, I had no idea where my career path would take me. But I wouldn't change a day of it.

Likewise, the 'Feast or Famine' project has been a roller-coaster journey of discovery and of self-discovery. This book prompted me to look back on life's incredible voyage and even, at times, explore again some of the darker places I visited before I started cooking.

I found myself immersed in the culture, music and food of those I was researching. I imagined how they had lived – how they had eaten and drunk, sown and reaped and cooked down through the centuries.

I followed the steps of the first Scots-Irish settlers from the North West who brought our food and culture to the New World. I found myself fascinated by the pioneering Getty family from the banks of the River Faughan who went on to help shape America. And I

I am passing on the McCourt family food heritage to our own wee budding chefs: Danaé and Luke (above) and Georgia (below) pictured with her grandmother Dorothy Armstrong. I hope they will do the same when the time comes with their own families and that this publication will help them in maintaining this proud tradition.

I would like to thank my partner Mary for her great support and patience over the years as I have pur-sued the stories at the heart of *Feast or Famine*.

Left: My grandfather Walter Marcum was a US Navy officer. His daughter Angela McCourt, née McCloskey, is pictured below.

Left: My father Denis McCourt with his new-season potatoes. Below: Denis and Angela with baby Danaé in 2005.

discovered why emigrants from this very region fought on both sides of the American Civil War.

The horrors of Ireland's Great Famine – the failures that led to it and prolonged it – are also central to this book. I gathered many testimonies of damage, pain and shame. I discovered how once-staple crops like the lumper potato were wrongly stigmatised and almost became extinct. But I also got to revisit the many heroes who helped the Irish poor, like the Choctaw Nation of America, The Society of Friends and the great Alexis Soyer.

Through the research I developed a huge understanding of what it was to be Irish through the centuries; the importance of the hearth; the heartbreak of land-loss and dispossession; the pain of emigration; and the ache as identity was eroded. I learned what it was to leave these shores never to return and to watch your culture dissolved into a melting pot. But ultimately, this culture will always re-emerge; and I was able, via genealogy and oral testimonies, to chart the massive contribution made to food heritage worldwide by those who left the North West of Ireland.

In many ways, those emigrant journeys mirrored my own as a chef when I left to work my way around the world on transoceanic cruise ships. And I would make my own very personal discoveries in far-flung lands. Through this project I would find my own grandfather – Walter Marcum – who served in Derry during World War II as a US Navy officer. I also found the many relatives I never knew in Virginia and Kentucky. And thus I found closure to more than 50 years of unanswered questions for my mother.

I spent many years travelling the world working in cruise-liner kitchens – but my passion was always for the food and heritage of my homeland.

Most of all, I discovered just how much our food heritage unites us and connects us with people and places across the globe. It marks our identity and allows the Irish to take their rightful place among the finest cuisines of the world.

I have always been inspired by County Derry man and world famous Nobel Laureate Seamus Heaney who sadly passed in 2013. His poems *Potato Digging* and *Picking Blackberries* infused me with a lasting passion for food and a strong pride in our land and our culinary tradition.

So, let me invite you now on this culinary odyssey, the start of an exciting food journey, which traces the food heritage and food culture of the people of the North West of Ireland.

I will endeavour to highlight our many food heroes and champion the people who have endured and struggled, through poverty and emigration, to preserve the North West's food heritage and traditional way of life.

This is their story, too.

Emmett McCourt
North West Regional College
Director, Irish Food Heritage Project

> The joys of the table belong equally to all ages,
> countries, conditions and times; they mix with all
> other pleasures and remain the last to console us
> for their loss.
>
> *Jean Anthelme Brillat-Savarin (1755–1826)*
> *French lawyer, politician, epicure and gastronome*

CHAPTER 1

Colmcille, the Vikings and the Chieftains (600—1600)

The trees that give Derry its name (*Doire* is the Irish for oak grove) are thought to have first flourished about 5,000 years ago, after the last Ice Age. But archaeologists believe that hunter-gatherers had been operating in the region since even before then, in the Mesolithic era (c.7000–4000 BC). The first recorded settlement on the banks of the River Foyle, however, dates back no further than the 6th century, when a monastery was established, purportedly by the city's patron saint, Colmcille (though other authorities have it as St Fiachra).

Colmcille, who was from neighbouring Donegal, would have found an abundant source of salmon and oysters in the Foyle. Indeed, these natural resources sustain an industry in the North West of Ireland to this very day, and the first monks would have been well versed in smoke-preserving fish for the winter months – there's evidence this process was well advanced in Ireland by this stage.

Irish legend, incidentally, teaches us that fish is good for the brain. The famed Gaelic adventurer Fionn Mac Cumhaill, when tasked to cook the much sought-after 'Salmon of Knowledge' for his master, Finnegas, inadvertently tasted it when he burnt his thumb and soothed it in his mouth. In doing so, Fionn gained all the knowledge there was in the world – and for the rest of his life he could learn anything he needed just by biting his thumb.

The early medieval diet, if records are accurate, was quite varied. Most food would, typically, have been cooked in a pit filled with

St Colmcille, patron saint of Derry.

boiling water, called a *fulacht fia*. Beef was rarely eaten, as cattle were reserved primarily for milking; pig flesh was preferred. Wild boars were native to Ireland's woodlands, though the 10th-century annals record that pigs were domesticated. Bacon fat was used in medieval recipes as it still is today.

Small pits such as this *fulacht fia* were used extensively throughout Ireland to cook meat.

St Columba statue by Niall Bruton in
St Columb's Park, Waterside, Derry.

By the 6th century, cows were being widely cultivated for their milk. Livestock was a measure of wealth and cattle-raiding was commonplace: it was seen as a rite of passage. Indeed, rustling is central to the most famous epic in ancient Irish literature, The Cattle Raid of Cooley (*Táin Bó Cuailnge*). Interestingly, until recent generations, milking and care of poultry would have been the sole preserve of women in Ireland because of their 'smaller hands'.

Venison has been eaten in Ireland from the Bronze Age, traditionally by the higher castes. Pits for roasting deer, dating back thousands of years, have been found all over the country. Poaching killed off much of the stock in the 18th and 19th centuries, but red deer were successfully re-introduced into Donegal a number of years ago.

Our ancestors were clearly fond of their poultry, too. Geese and hens both merit inclusion in the *Book of Kells* (c.800), while ancient Brehon Laws (700–800) spell out fines for domestic fowl which damage neighbouring property.

The Brehon Laws also reference medicinal vegetables and herbs, thought to have been the likes of onion and parsley. And the annals also mention root vegetables, possibly rutabagas (turnips), which would have been cultivated and eaten with cake or dry bread. Wheat, barley and oats were farmed widely.

The Normans are credited with introducing peas, beans and other pulse in the late 12th century. And they also developed meat-curing methods, using salt from burnt seaweed as a preservative, which led to trade links with France. Before then, beef and pork may have been buried in peat bogs to preserve it.

Mead and ale would both have been produced locally. And wine had already been popular in Ireland for centuries. Furs, hides and salted meat would have been traded with the Gauls for barrels of the grape drink.

'Red Stag'. Wild deer were plentiful throughout the North West until poaching devastated stocks in the 18th and 19th centuries. (Courtesy John R Moore, Irish wildlife and sporting artist.)

Baking cakes and bread is an age-old Irish tradition and predates the first records, with references to flour sieving and baking techniques appearing in Brehon texts. Indeed, according to Brehon Law, it was incumbent upon foster parents to teach their female charges baking skills.

Colmcille's monks may have had access to apples, blackberries, raspberries, sloes, strawberries and whortleberries. These may have been sweetened with honey farmed from bees. And for breakfast, it's known that, from the 9th century, there was a type of muesli, derived from raw cereals and hazelnuts, which would have been eaten with honey and milk.

The Vikings, meanwhile, get credit for introducing rhubarb, which was to become an Irish staple. They are also credited with teaching the Celts fishing techniques and their method of curing fish. Viking influence on ship design can be seen to this day in the structure of modern Irish fishing vessels such as the Drontheim or the Greencastle Yawl.

Early condiments would have included dulse – a versatile seaweed, light green or crimson in colour – which can still be found dried out and sold in shops. Dulse, which is rich in potassium and magnesium, is often used to enhance the flavour of other foods like potatoes, oatcakes or bread. Shell dulse (*creathnach*) is an even more highly prized delicacy and is usually found in the company of small mussels along the shorelines of the North West and rocky outcrops off Inishowen.

The *Book of Kells,* sometimes referred to as the *Book of Columba* (Colmcille).

Dulse, a ruby-red-coloured seaweed, was often used in early recipes for its naturally salty flavour and its much vaunted nutritional value.

Derry has many areas, churches and items of interest named after Colmcille.

Loin of Venison with Blackberry, Celeriac Purée, Potato Fondant and Baby Carrots

Ingredients (Serves 4)

1kg venison loin, trimmed
1 quarter of celeriac, peeled and chopped
200ml cream
1 glass of port
200ml game or beef gravy
1 small onion, diced
4 large potatoes, peeled
150ml chicken stock
500g baby carrots, washed, peeled and boiled
100g butter, diced
50ml melted butter
Broighter Gold rapeseed oil for frying
200g blackberries
salt and pepper to season

Method

For the Venison

1. Wrap the venison loin in clingfilm and tie at both ends to form a sausage shape.
2. Leave to set in fridge.
3. Slice the venison into steaks through the clingfilm.
4. Season the venison with salt and pepper on both sides.
5. In a non-stick pan, add the rapeseed oil and heat until smoking.
6. Remove clingfilm and panfry the venison on both sides and cook to your liking.
7. You may retain the juices in the pan for the sauce.
8. Finish in the oven if preferred.

For the Blackberry Sauce

1. In the pan, add a knob of diced butter and fry the diced onions gently, without adding colour, stirring the base of the pan to retain the venison sediment.
2. Add the port and simmer to deglaze the pan of meat juices.
3. Reduce by half by simmering and then add the blackberries and gravy. Reduce further until the sauce is slightly thickened.
4. Add a knob of cold diced butter and whisk in to glaze the sauce before serving.

For the Baby Carrots

1. Boil to cook and keep warm until serving.

For the Celeriac Purée

1. In a saucepan, sweat the chopped celeriac in butter.
2. Add the cream, bring to the boil, turn down the heat and simmer until soft.
3. Season with salt and pepper.
4. Add the cooked celeriac and cream to a blender. Blend until a fine purée is achieved.
5. Pass through a sieve and reheat before serving with the venison.

For the Fondant Potatoes

1. Season the potatoes with salt and pepper and slice to shape with a circular cutter.
2. Fry the shaped potatoes in a non-stick pan with the rapeseed oil and a knob of butter, until golden brown.
3. Add the melted butter and chicken stock.
4. Cook on top of the stove or in the oven. Baste occasionally until tender.

Peter Gott
Wild-Boar Farmer and
a Man with a Mission

I first met Peter Gott at the Great Game Fairs of Ireland in 2008. He has been exhibiting his wild-boar produce at food shows in Ireland for almost 30 years. Peter has a great passion for food heritage and how it links cultures around the world. He is a great character and without doubt one of the best artisan producers and farmers on these islands.

Originally from a farming and retail background, Peter first became interested in wild-boar rare-breed pig production in 1993, when his brother gave him four wild-boar gilts as a joke. Since then he has greatly developed this specialist business at Sillfield Farm in Cumbria. It has about eighteen acres of coniferous woodland which is an ideal habitat for wild boar. He now has about 150 wild boar stock originating mainly from German and Belgian lines, as well as some breeding stock with Russian blood in them. Wild boar are reared on conventional pig-feed, but all additives and growth promoters are excluded.

In order to promote his business and learn ever more about the food industry, Peter attends various food fairs and festivals, mainly in Britain and Ireland, but also abroad. He now rents permanent stall space at London's world-famous Borough Market, close to London Bridge. In 1994, Sillfield Farm won the 'Best Market Stall Award' out of over 300 market traders at the Dutch International Market in Den Bosch.

Peter is a member of the National Market Traders Federation and helped to set up the Southern Irish Market and Street Traders Association. He strongly believes in the Slow Food movement, which encourages and promotes local food and artisan food production, and is involved with the promotion of quality food and food production through the media having appeared on numerous TV and radio shows.

He is a strong supporter of the Irish Food Heritage Project and we are proud to celebrate the diversity of food produce and culinary expertise which Peter brings to the table. If you want to watch him at work or sample any of his famous artisan pies, he regularly attends the Great Game Fairs of Ireland – so don't miss your opportunity.

Peter sees himself as a 'Man with a Mission', who works very hard not only to keep his business successful, but also to bring inspiration and enthusiasm to all those with whom he works and associates.

As he firmly believes, and often states: 'Good food, after all, is one of the greatest pleasures in life.'

Wild boar was commonly eaten throughout medieval Ireland and Peter Gott is pioneering a revival of this tradition with his range of succulent artisan boar pies.

CHAPTER 2

Plantation and the Pratie Boom (1600s)

In the late 16th century, English troops arrived in northwest Ireland by land and sea to quell the 'rebellious' Gaelic chieftain Shane O'Neill. They used the ancient monastic settlement of Derry as their base, but in 1567 their camp (and virtually the entire town) was burned to the ground, following a fire at an ammunition store. In 1600, a new expedition led by Sir Henry Docwra saw the English begin to resettle in the area, and in 1604 King James I issued a charter for the new city of 'Derrie'.

Stained glass from Derry's Guildhall commemorating the founding of the city.

After the Flight of the Earls in 1607, when northern Irish chieftains opposed to English rule fled to the continent, King James claimed the six 'escheated' counties of Armagh, Cavan, Coleraine (later Derry), Tyrconnell (Donegal), Fermanagh and Tyrone. London merchants were then coerced into sponsoring the 'Plantation' of these areas, a process in which Scottish and English tenants would settle on the confiscated land in an attempt to 'pacify' and 'civilise the natives'.

The new walled city of London-Derry was then established (1613–17), under the aegis of a newly formed organisation called The Honourable The Irish Society, and quickly became the region's capital. Smaller plantation towns were also developed in nearby Limavady, Newtowncunningham, Raphoe, Newtownstewart, Omagh and Coleraine.

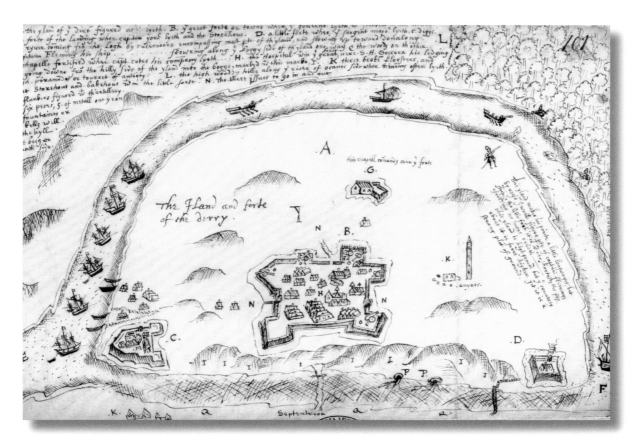

A sketch map recording Henry Docwra's original fortifications in Derry in 1600.

The region to be colonised – which was referred to as O'Cahan's Country – was selected because of its tremendous natural resources and, in particular, the huge potential for fishing, agriculture and forestry. There was an abundance of arable land and cattle. And major rivers such as the Foyle and the Bann boasted massive stocks of salmon and eel.

George Hill, in his book *The Conquest of Ireland: An Historical Account of the Plantation of Ulster at the Commencement of the Seventeenth Century* (1877), outlines 'The Commodities with which the North of Ireland Affords':

The country is well watered and supplied with fuel either of trees or turf (peat). It supplies such abundance of provisions as may not only sustain the plantation but may furnish provisions yearly to the city of London, especially for their fleets, as beeves [cattle], pork, fish, rye, bere, peas, beans and in some years will help the dearth of the city and country about. It is fit for breeding of mares and for cattle and hence may be expected stores of hides and tallow. The soil is suited for English sheep. It is fit in many parts for madder, hops and woods. It affords fells of red deer, foxes, sheep and lambs, cony [rabbits], martens, squirrels. It grows hemp and flax better than elsewhere, and thus might furnish materials for canvas cables, cordage and such like requisites for shipping, also for thread linen clothes and stuffs made of linen yarn which is finer there and more plentiful than all the rest of the kingdom. Timber, stone, lime and slate and building materials are to be had, and the soil is good for making bricks and tiles.

Among the English merchants who constituted The Irish Society, which sustained the Plantation, were several London livery groups associated with the food industry. These included the Worshipful Companies of Fishmongers, Skinners, Salters and Distillers. And, while the farming methods of the mainly Scottish settlers wouldn't have been significantly more advanced than the indigenous Irish, their backers certainly brought new skills to the area.

LONDONDERRY
ABOUT 1850

PRESENTED BY THE
WORSHIPFUL COMPANY OF
SALTERS · LONDON · 1913

CHARTER
A.D 1473
GRANTED

PRESENTED BY
THE WORSHIPFUL COMPANY OF PEWTERERS
LONDON A.D. 1911

Lecturer in Food Production at the Dublin Institute of Technology John Linnane, in his 2000 tract *A History of Irish Cuisine*, says any attempt to record the history of 'pre-potato' cuisine should start with the use of the cauldron, 'a large three-legged pot', which hung over the fire and simmered continuously. He writes:

> Depending on whether the community was inland or coastal would determine the types of foods chosen for cauldron cooking. Coastal communities collected a variety of shellfish (razorbills, cockles, clams, oysters, limpets, periwinkles, mussels, prawns and crabs), added seaweed, some herbs and vegetables to make a soup/stew, which was left simmering for hours then eaten with oat bread (O'Brien Education, 1972). Meat and game were also cooked in this fashion. Necessity having been the mother of invention, the cauldron inspired Irish cooks to devise endless pottage and soups such as Irish farm broth, sheep's head broth, clam and cockle soup, hot lobster soup, just to name a few (Sexton, 1998).

The advent of the potato in Ireland was to change the culinary landscape hugely, however. The crop first arrived in the country in the late 1500s. The English explorer Walter Raleigh (1552–1618) brought back seed potatoes from America and cultivated them in his Myrtle Grove estate outside Cork. But there is an interesting theory that potatoes may have been grown in Donegal before then, having been washed ashore from the wrecks of a number of Spanish Armada ships, which sank off the northwest coast of Ireland in 1588.

The Spanish first 'discovered' the potato when they arrived in Peru in 1532 in search of gold and are credited with introducing the crop to Europe. Pedro de Cieza de Leon (1518–60), Spanish conquistador and historian, wrote about the potato in his accounts, *Chronicles of Peru*, in 1540:

> In the vicinities of Quito, the inhabitants have with the maize another plant that serves to support in great part their existence: the potatoes, that they are of the roots similar to the tubercoli … when they come bubbled they become to hold like the cooked chestnuts.

John Linnane argues that, although the vegetable had been grown in the Americas for thousands of years, Ireland was the first country to seriously consider it as a staple food. By the mid-1600s, the potato was cultivated and eaten widely here, becoming the centrepiece of the winter diet, and by the 18th century it was known as the 'Irish' potato. One of the reasons for the prevalence of the potato, particularly among the indigenous Irish, was that the crop could be grown on poor or boggy land. This proved to be an important attribute as the planters had assumed ownership of the best arable land.

Linnane notes that the nourishing qualities of potatoes helped the 17th-century Irish survive harsh winters. He quotes Redcliffe Salaman, an expert in potato cultivation, from *The History and Social Influence of the Potato* (Cambridge University Press, 1949):

> The new diet of potato and oatmeal was regarded by the Irish as inferior but was nutritious and allowed the population to increase even during the Little Ice Age of 1650 to 1720. Indeed, Ireland's population would increase from less than a million in the late 1500s to 8.2 million by 1840 as the country's food resources rose dramatically.

Summer Salad of Smoked Lough Neagh Eel with Roasted Beetroot, Walnut, Celeriac and Broighter Gold Rapeseed Oil Dressing

Ingredients (Serves 4)

400g smoked Lough Neagh eel cut into
3 diamond slices
2 whole beetroot
100g walnuts, chopped
100g celeriac, peeled and grated
50g horseradish, peeled and grated
2 tbsp of mayonnaise
1 tsp Dijon mustard
1 tbsp white vinegar
1 tsp sugar
a drop of lemon juice
summer salad leaves – wild rocket, oak leaf,
red chard, mustard leaves
edible flowers, rapeseed, chive, borage,
nasturtiums
salt and pepper to season
100ml Broighter Gold rapeseed oil

Method

For the Roasted Beetroot

1. Prepare the beetroot for roasting by washing thoroughly in cold water.

2. Slice the stalk and root from the beetroot and pierce with a knife several times.

3. Season with rock salt and wrap in tinfoil.

4. Roast in moderate oven at 180C/Gas 4 for 1¼ hours and allow to cool.

For the Walnut and Roasted Beetroot

1. Skin, slice and dice one roasted beetroot.

2. Mix with the chopped walnuts.

3. Add Broighter Gold rapeseed oil to bind and add a little sugar and season to taste.

For the Broighter Gold and Beetroot Dressing

1. Skin and chop the remaining beetroot and liquidise or blend, adding the vinegar and sugar.

2. Season with salt and pepper.

3. Turn the liquidiser to low speed, slowly adding the Broighter Gold rapeseed oil.

4. Liquidise until a fine dressing is achieved, adding more oil if necessary.

For the Celeriac Remoulade

1. Mix the grated celeriac and horseradish in a bowl.

2. Add the lemon juice and Dijon mustard and bind with the mayonnaise.

3. Season to taste.

Finish and Present

1. Panfry or grill the smoked Lough Neagh eel for 2 minutes on each side.

2. Arrange the celeriac remoulade on the centre of the plate.

3. Add a little dressing to the salad leaves and arrange on top of the celeriac.

4. Place the cooked eel on top of the salad.

5. Spoon a little of the walnut and beetroot mixture on top of the eel and around the plate.

6. Drizzle with the dressing. Finish by arranging the edible flowers on and around the plate.

This Window Presented
Governor Of

To The City
The Honou

CHAPTER 3

Surviving the Siege

(1630—1700)

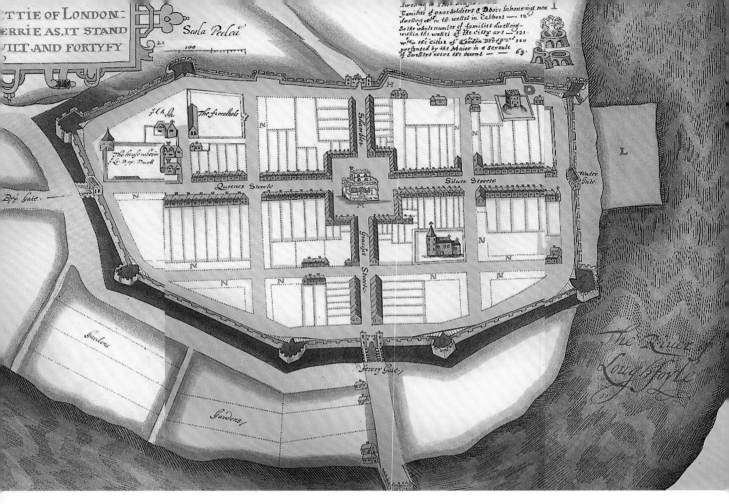

The walled city of Derry in the mid-17th century.

Most of the Scots who moved to Derry and east Donegal prior to 1630 were the Scots Redshanks (Highland Scots) and Ayrshire Scots. The movement of other east Lowland Scots into these areas did not happen until later. Their first task was to build fortresses and walled enclosures of their settlements to protect the planters and their cattle from the native Irish. The constructions they built were called bawns, from the Gaelic *bó dhún* – cow fort. The Irish had traditionally used blackthorn fences to protect their cattle.

Following the Cattle Acts in the mid-17th century, livestock became a huge economic commodity for Ireland. Salted (or 'corned') beef became a major export through the Port of Londonderry. This subsequently led to the city developing into a port of major sig-

nificance, building up extensive trade connections with Britain, Europe and the colonies in North America. According to Brian Mitchell, in *The Making of Derry: An Economic History* (1992), Derry had a population of 500 adult males by 1630, in comparison to Coleraine which had 300 and Strabane with 200. He writes:

At this stage, the Plantation of Ulster compared favourably with that of America. Derry was very similar in size to Boston, which in 1640 had a population of 1,200. New York had some 400 people, making it smaller than Strabane in 1640.

The success of the emerging city of Derry brought its own perils. When war for the English throne broke out in 1688, the native Irish

Derry's Gates were closed against the Jacobite army and the walled city was besieged for 105 days.

allied themselves with the ousted King James II, a Catholic, as they believed he would return their confiscated lands; the Protestant planters in Derry sided with William of Orange.

In 1688, James raised an army of mostly Irish and French troops and marched on Derry. On 18 April 1689, a siege began which lasted 105 days, during which around 10,000 people died inside the Walls, from disease, starvation and the heavy shelling. The Jacobite army, in turn, lost some 9,000 troops from battle and disease, before fleeing from the advancing Williamites, who broke through a boom on the River Foyle and retook the city.

Up to 30,000 civilians and troops from all over Plantation Ulster had crowded into the walled city (normal population 2,000) at the outset of the siege, and they were forced to eat all manner of things to survive. They were further disadvantaged as their former governor, Robert Lundy, had fled the city after allowing the bulk of the city's stores to fall into the enemy's hands.

The new siege museum on Derry's Walls provides a fascinating insight into how desperate the situation became. According to records there, by the time the siege ended on 31 July 1689, there were only nine lean horses left alive in the city – the rest had been eaten. Indeed, a butcher's menu from the time shows rats which had been 'fed on human flesh' were being sold for 1s.0d each, while a quarter of a dog, 'fattened by eating corpses', went for 5s.6d:

The Siege Menu

A quart of meal: 1s. 0d
One pound of horseflesh: 1s. 8d
One pound of tallow: 4s. 0d
One pound of salted hides: 1s. 0d
One pound of greaves [rendered animal-fat]: 1s. 0d
¼ of a dog (fattened by eating corpses): 5s. 6d
A dog's head: 2s. 6d
A quart of horse blood: 1s. 0d
A horse's pudding (gut): 0s. 6d
A cat: 4s. 6d
A rat fed on human flesh: 1s. 0d
A mouse: 0s. 6d
A handful of sea wrack [seaweed]: 0s. 2d
A handful of chickweed: 0s. 1d

Soldiers and defenders of the city had a daily allowance of ½lb of meal, ½lb of shelled oats and ½lb dry salted hides. According to the archive, water 'as could be found' was mainly contaminated.

Derry was devastated by the siege, and the rebuilding was a slow process, hampered by the failure of the London parliament to compensate the city's defenders and citizens. Presbyterians, in particular, felt they got little credit for the role they had played.

Shortly after the siege, Penal Laws, which attempted to force Catholics and Presbyterians to convert to the Church of Ireland, were enacted. And this, in turn, led to a wave of emigration from the North West in the early 1700s.

One of the surviving defenders of the city, interestingly, was a man called James Getty, who was, it is believed, the head of the Getty family which travelled in the 18th century to America and later founded Gettysburg.

A Carrot by any Other Colour

The modern orange carrot was developed and promoted by some Dutch growers around the beginning of the seventeenth century. Legend had it that it was cultivated with that particular colour to honour William of Orange.

However, although the orange carrot can indeed be traced back to the Netherlands, it is now thought unlikely that its colouring had anything to do with King William.

The romantic myth was that Dutch farmers worked on a random unexpected mutation especially to give tribute to King William I for leading the Dutch revolt against the Spanish to gain independence from Spain. But there is no documentary evidence for this story!

Surviving on Tallow Pancakes

The following testimony from survivors of the siege appeared in a book published in Londonderry, New Hampshire, a town founded by Scots-Irish emigrants from the North West on the east coast of America:

By the middle of June, the besieged began to suffer for the want of provision and were reduced to the necessity of salting and eating the flesh of the horses that were killed in the various skirmishes about the city. They obtained a temporary supply by digging up cellars and other places, where they found considerable quantities of meal and other provision, which had been buried by those who had died or left the city. But they had the prospect of famine before their eyes if they continued the defence unless speedy relief should be sent them.

During the month of July, the most extreme distress was felt from the scarcity of provisions: many died from starvation and the garrison was reduced to eating the vilest and most unwholesome food. Horse flesh, cats, dogs, rats and salted hides were eaten. Tallow (rendered animal fat), which they humorously called 'French butter', was mixed with meal, ginger, pepper and anise seeds, and in this way, what they considered excellent pancakes were made. Towards the latter part of the month, a quantity of starch was discovered in one of the storehouses. This, mixed with tallow, was found to be not only a valuable article of food but a remedy for dysentery which at that time prevailed.

The History of Londonderry, Comprising the Towns of Derry and Londonderry, NH, by Rev Edward Lutwyche Parker (1851).

Derry~Londonderry in revolutionary times – a Georgian Banquet

The Irish Food Heritage Project was commissioned by Holywell Trust (Walled City Project) to re-create an authentic Georgian banquet with the aid of Northern Period Productions, a professional living history company specialising in staging historical presentations. The menu included syllabub (a period dessert), salamongundy (a fresh salad) and quail.

FROM PIONEERS
TO PRESIDENTS
"My Ulster blood is my most priceless heritage..."
PRESIDENT JAMES BUCHANAN
15TH US PRESIDENT, 1857-1861
INGTON ST

SCOTCH-IRISH SETTLEMENT

In April 1719, sixteen Presbyterian Scotch-Irish families settled here in two rows of cabins along West Running Brook easterly of Beaver Brook. Initially known as Nutfield, the settlement became Londonderry in 1723. The first year, a field was planted, known as the Common Field, where the potato was first grown in North America.

CHAPTER 4

Taking Irish Cuisine to the New World (1700s)

> **"My forefathers were... the men who had followed Cromwell and who shared in the defence of Derry, and in the victories of Aughrim and the Boyne..."**
>
> PRESIDENT THEODORE ROOSEVELT.
> 26TH US PRESIDENT, 1901-1904

Many world-renowned American icons, politicians, entertainers and business pioneers can trace their roots back to the early Scots-Irish immigrants including several US Presidents, Bill Gates, Neil Armstrong, John Wayne and Davy Crockett. Even 'The King' himself – Elvis Presley – is believed to have Scots-Irish ancestry.

More than a quarter of a million Scots-Irish would embark for America from the North West of Ireland during the 18th century, taking their cultures, foods and farming skills with them. Many of those first emigrants were descendants of the planters who fought in the Siege of Derry; a few were actually veterans. They believed if they could survive one of the bloodiest battles in Irish history, they could prevail anywhere. Among those who ventured to the New World from this region were the forebears of future US presidents Andrew Jackson and Woodrow Wilson (whose family came from Strabane), and frontiersmen like Davy Crockett (from Donemana).

The first mass exodus of the Scots-Irish occurred in 1718 as a result of the Penal Laws. Six ships set off with passengers emanating from Donegal, Derry, Coleraine and 'the Foyle and Bann districts'. Led by County Derry minister James McGregor, son of Captain McGregor of Magilligan, they arrived in Boston on 4 August 1718 before going on to establish Londonderry in New Hampshire (the neighbouring settlement of Derry, home to poet Robert Frost, would get its town charter a century later).

The land the settlers encountered was inhabited by Native Americans from the Merrimack tribe and was largely uncultivated. The natives were very hospitable and taught the visitors how to catch salmon and shad (herring) with homemade nets and how to catch lobster in pots.

For the first few years, until their own crops took hold, the colonists found the going hard and, initially, they adopted the local diet of corn and beans, along with nuts and wild fruit.

When corn and beans were cooked together, the dish was called succotash. Hominy was made by pounding dry corn in a mortar with a stone pestle until it was made into coarse meal, which was then boiled. Baked beans, one of New England's signature dishes (Boston is known as 'Beantown'), were first produced by the Native Americans. And they also made corn cake, baking it on flat rocks before the fire. In summer, they gave the settlers' children popcorn, which the natives called 'the corn that flowers'.

Spuds, Apples and Moonshine

The biggest single change that the North West settlers would bring to the New World diet – and one which would immediately proliferate across the colonies – was the introduction of the potato as a staple food. Attempts to cultivate the crop had been made in America several times during the 1600s but had failed every time. The potato was regarded as an unfit food.

McGregor's followers, however, had brought large quantities of local potato seed in their ships and, in 1719, a crop of potatoes was grown in what was then the Derry region of Londonderry NH. Thanks to the skill of the Scots-Irish settlers, the crop was a major success and word spread quickly that potatoes were a nutritious and tasty food source. Potatoes were soon being cultivated right across the colonies.

Birthplace of First Irish white Potato
PATTEN • MURDOCK • WHITE
The First Irish Potatoes grown In North America were planted HERE during the spring of 1719 by the Early Settlers of Nutfield (Londonderry) now Derry, N.H., on the Common Field bordering West Running Brook.

Burt Potato King

Ulster-Scots historians credit the Young family from Burt, just outside Derry, with introducing the Irish potato to North America. The potato which Walter Raleigh is said to have brought to Europe from America in the 16th century was the sweet potato – a totally different plant.

In 1718, the Youngs settled in Worcester, 40 miles west of Boston, and a monument to the family's patriarch, designed by his son William, still stands there to this day. It reads: 'Here lies interred the remains of John Young, who was born in the Isle of Bert [sic] near Londonderry, in the Kingdom of Ireland. He departed this life on 30 June 1730, aged 107 years.' (*The Ulster-Scots & New England*, Alister McReynolds, 2010.)

Another Derry claim to fame, according to Rev Edward Lutwyche Parker's history of Londonderry, NH, is the introduction to America of apple pie, the country's signature dish. Those first settlers from Ireland also brought apple trees to 'new' Londonderry. These trees would thrive into massive orchards, and the first apple pie originated from the region. One of New Hampshire's major tourism attractions to this day is a 10-mile stretch of orchard groves planted by the Scots-Irish settlers from Derry. It is known as 'The Apple Way'. Robert Frost's seminal poem *After Apple-Picking* was also written about the region.

The third major agricultural contribution the first settlers to Londonderry brought was flax seed, along with the spinning wheel and the skilled art of manufacturing linen. It quickly became apparent that the linen of Londonderry was of a superior quality, that it was sought after the world over and that it commanded a higher price. Inferior linens bearing the name 'Derry' spread throughout the market place, so to prevent fraud, the town decreed that all linen manufactured in the area must carry a stamp, and only be sold with a certificate of authenticity. Londonderry linen was soon in demand in New England and in Europe and was worn by both George Washington and Thomas Jefferson.

A less salubrious but nonetheless very popular addition to the colonies was Irish whiskey, and the new settlers were masters at manufacturing the drink. Foremost among the craftsmen were the Scots-Irish who settled in the Appalachians. Former *poitín* makers in the Old Country, they produced corn whiskey, the quality of which was unrivalled anywhere. It was to become known as 'moonshine'.

The new immigrants found the English colonial government just as unpalatable as they had in their homeland, so the sparsely populated Southern Appalachian Mountains suited them well. As they were still loyal to King William of Orange at that time, they were nicknamed the 'Hill Billies'.

After Apple-Picking

My long two-pointed ladder's sticking through a tree
Toward heaven still,
And there's a barrel that I didn't fill
Beside it, and there may be two or three
Apples I didn't pick upon some bough.
But I am done with apple-picking now.
Essence of winter sleep is on the night,
The scent of apples; I am drowsing off.
Robert Frost (*North of Boston*, 1915).

Frost (1874–1963) lived in Derry, New Hampshire, on a farm gifted to him by his grandparents, close to the apple plantations cultivated by Scots-Irish settlers. His farm is now a National Monument.

Traditional Irish Apple Tart

This traditional apple tart recipe is quick and easy and ensures a perfect result every time. Use cooking or Bramley apples for the best filling. The dough can also be made in a food processor by mixing the flour, butter, sugar, and salt in the bowl of the processor on a pulse setting. When the mixture resembles breadcrumbs, add the egg, slowly, through the funnel until the dough comes together in a ball. Wrap in clingfilm and chill.

Ingredients (Serves 8)

Sugar Pastry
250g all purpose/plain flour
pinch of salt
60g caster sugar
145g butter, cubed
1-2 medium-sized eggs, beaten

Filling
700g cooking apples, peeled, cored and quartered
2 tbsp lemon juice
160g sugar
1 tsp ground cinnamon (optional) or 1 tsp ground cloves (optional)
25g butter
milk to glaze

Method

1. Place the flour, butter and salt into a large bowl. Rub the butter into the flour with your fingertips until the mixture resembles fine breadcrumbs, working as quickly as possible to prevent the dough becoming warm.

2. Add the egg to the mixture and, using a cold knife, stir until the dough binds together. Add a little cold water, a teaspoon at a time, if the mixture is too dry.

3. Wrap the dough in clingfilm and chill for between 15-30 minutes.

4. Preheat the oven to 180C/Gas 4.

5. Meanwhile, simmer the apples with the lemon juice and butter in a large pan with lid until slightly soft, but not puréed, and leave to cool. Add the sugar and cinnamon/cloves to the cooked apples when cold.

6. Roll out half the pastry and line a 17cm lightly buttered oven-proof plate. Put the cooled, cooked apple mixture into the pastry case.

7. Roll out the remaining pastry to make a lid for the tart. Damp the edges of the pastry in the dish with a little cold water, cover with the lid and press the edges firmly together and crimp the edges to decorate.

8. Brush the top of the pie with milk and bake at the top of a hot oven for 20-25 minutes.

9. Serve hot or cold with cream, ice cream or custard.

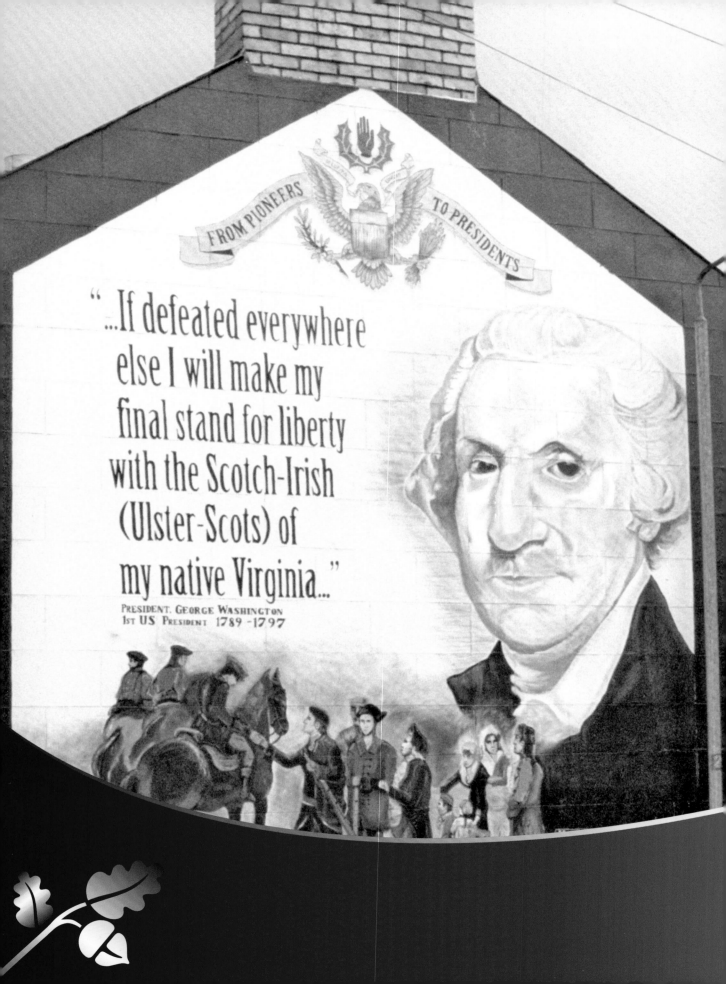

> Ireland, thou friend of my country in my country's most friendless days, much injured, much enduring land, accept this poor tribute from one who esteems thy worth, and mourns thy desolation.
>
> *George Washington, on Ireland's support for America during the revolution.*

LINCOLN ADDRESS MEMORIAL

This monument commemorates Lincoln's Gettysburg Address, November 19, 1863.

The Address was delivered about 300 yards from this spot along the upper Cemetery drive. The site is now marked by the Soldiers' National Monument.

Dedicated Jan. 24, 1912 - Sculptor: Henry Bush-Brown

CHAPTER 5

Feeding the Founding Fathers (1800s)

The mass exodus of the Scots-Irish continued throughout the 18th century until the American Revolution of 1776. The later immigrants started to travel further inland and further south. They established trails and settlements in the Shenandoah Valley of Virginia, the highlands of northwest Carolina, and portions of central and eastern Kentucky. Others moved further west to Pennsylvania, Ohio, Indiana and beyond. And, as previously mentioned, a substantial number of Scots-Irish settled in the Appalachian area, where they honed their whiskey-making skills.

There were some significant success stories. In the early 1820s, like tens of thousands before them, William, James and Jane McCain from Castlefin in Donegal made the trip across the Atlantic and settled in New Brunswick in Canada. After a few years working as labourers, all three obtained 100-acre land grants near Florenceville and began trading farm produce. Less than 200 years on, the settlers' heirs run McCain Foods, the world's biggest producer of French fries. So, amazingly, a third of all frozen chips sold across the globe today are of Donegal descent!

In an interview with the *Finn Valley People* in 2000, the company's former chairman Harrison McCain said the family's 'Irish character' lay behind their success. He explained: 'Definitely permeating the Irish – and also permeating the McCain family – is a love of the land. It is an inherited love for owning the land, and being in an agricultural environment, and trading farm produce and farming. That's what our ancestors came from, and they definitely had a liking for it.'

The McIlhennys from Milford, who emigrated in the early 1800s, would also make their mark on the world's culinary landscape. In 1868, Edmund, a banker who had settled in Louisiana, invented a hot sauce which he sold in old cologne bottles branded as 'McIlhenny's Chili Pepper Shrub'. The taste caught on and Edmund's invention is today sold across the globe as Tabasco sauce. A descendant of Edmund, Henry McIlhenny, later purchased Glenveagh Castle in Donegal, where he hosted parties for the likes of Greta Garbo and Grace Kelly. On his death in 1981, Henry bequeathed the house and grounds to the Irish State, which today runs the facility as a National Park (below).

Another enterprising family who pulled themselves up by their bootstraps were the Gettys, a Scots-Irish clan who hailed from Eglinton. Samuel Gettys left the Port of Londonderry in 1740 and travelled to Pennsylvania, where he and his descendants founded the town of Gettysburg, the site of President Abraham Lincoln's landmark speech in 1863. Samuel's descendant John Paul Getty became an oil magnate and industrialist, and was worth some $4 billion at the time of his death in 1976.

In Memory Of
Samuel Gettys
d. Mar. 15, 1790
and wife
Isabella Ramsey Gettys
d. Mar. 12, 1815 age 84yrs.
Scotch-Irish pioneer settlers
and storekeepers
• • • • • • • • • •
Dedicated by Descendants of
their son, William Gettys
1998

A dedication to Samuel Gettys, one of the founding fathers of Gettysburg in the USA.

The Faughan Connection

The River Faughan ('sheltered place') holds a very special place in my heart. I spent a lot of time there as a youth learning the art of fly-fishing for trout and salmon. Over the years I met many great characters and friends who have lived and fished near the Faughan for generations, with fascinating stories of long-gone times.

In *Along the Faughan Side* by the late great naturalist and historian Olly McGilloway, Olly lists the testimonies of hundreds of people who have lived along its banks over the generations. One such meeting with local farmer Robert Lynch inspired me to research further the journey that Irish food heritage has taken to the new world.

In his interview, Robert Lynch (below right) claimed that the Gettys hailed from along the banks of the River Faughan and that he himself was their distant relative. I met with Robert in February 2013 and asked him about his links with famous American oil tycoon Jean Paul Getty.

He told me that it was his late grandfather's assertion that his family had passed down stories and histories of their proud connection to the Gettys and their exploits and success in America. He claimed that Mrs Getty's maiden name was Lynch (his great, great, great aunt). Robert also said there was a tradition of adding the Getty name to theirs over the generations (his uncle was named Ivan Getty-Lynch).

It is certainly true that the Gettys originated from around this area (now Lisneal) and that they may have lived near Ardnaguniog which had strong connections with the Lynch family. Robert then directed me to meet Richard Craig (below left) – of Ard House in the townland of Ardnaguniog – who had identified a stone dedication at his home connected to the Gettys.

The description on the stone says, 'erected by James Getty', so I presume that he was the man who built the house. Richard was always told that this James Getty was related to Jean Paul Getty. One of the past residents of Ard House was also William Getty-Lynch, a relation of James Getty. The Craigs are also believed to be distant relations of the Gettys, who have been farming in Ardnaguniog since the 1700s. Richard believes that several members of this Getty family subsequently emigrated to America in the 1800s to found the Getty dynasty.

It wasn't just the potato that the emigrants were being credited for. They were also said to have introduced seafood chowder to the east coast of America and Canada. The Huguenots originally brought the dish from France to Ulster. It later became popular for centuries with fishermen, particularly along Ireland's western shore, where it would have been cooked in a three-legged cauldron above a fire. Chowder is now, of course, one of New England's most well-known signature dishes.

In the early 1800s, the Scots-Irish brought across rhubarb to Massachusetts and Maine, where it quickly caught on, becoming known as 'pie plant'. Interestingly, some of the settlers also used rhubarb to make sweet wine. Hash browns, now a staple breakfast food across the US, were derived from 'boxty', the traditional Donegal pancake made from grated potatoes and beloved by the settlers. The Scots-Irish were also experts at curing meat: they had perfected salting techniques during the mid-17th century when live cattle exports from Ireland to Britain were banned.

The processes used in curing the beef in the 16th and 17th centuries are still found today. The beef was cut into 8lb pieces, graded, salted and cured in casks. The casks were left to stand for four or five days and then sealed by a cooper. The Irish only used the highest quality white dry salt in their curing process, and their 'corned' beef was to become a universally loved dish in the New World. Indeed, it was eaten by none other than President Abraham Lincoln on St Patrick's Day to celebrate his nation's links to the Old Country.

Corned (salted) beef was a huge export from back home in Ireland, too, and a major part of the country's global trade. Ships would bring salt beef and salted herrings from Ireland to the Caribbean. These would then bring rum from the West Indies to Virginia and New York before returning to Ireland, laden with flax seed for the Irish linen industry. According to historian Brian Mitchell, Derry exports to the American colonies and West Indies were on a par with the city's exports to Britain towards the end of the 18th century. Indeed, the Derry port's revenue quadrupled in the years from 1729 to 1767. And in 1771, for example, 215,000 yards of linen, 68 hundredweight of butter, 584 barrels of beef and 200 barrels of herring were shipped out of the port across the Atlantic.

The Boxty Song

Boxty on the griddle
Boxty in the Pan
If you can't make boxty
You'll never get your man.
(Traditional)

Farming Australia

In the 19th century, Australia would also become a final destination for thousands of Irish. There were those who were deported for crimes including sedition, as immortalised in the Bobby Sands song *Back Home in Derry*.

But in the 1830s, there was also a major recruitment drive to encourage farmers to travel to the Antipodes. The Londonderry Port website, in its section *Derry as an Emigration Port*, reports:

> Most emigrants from northwest Ireland destined for Australia, New Zealand or South Africa would have begun their journey on the cross-channel steamer out of Derry to either Glasgow or Liverpool.
>
> However, in the period 1837 to 1845,

the British Government fitted out ships to take selected emigrants from Irish ports such as Belfast, Cork, Derry and Limerick to New South Wales, Australia. Eligible emigrants and, in particular, 'married agriculturists, not exceeding a certain age, with their wives and families' were given a free passage.

In 1837 and 1838, three ships provided by the government – *Adam Lodge*, *Parland* and *Susan* – sailed direct from Derry for New South Wales with, in total, nearly 1,000 emigrants … with the selection process being 'confined to a certain distance into the Counties of Derry, Tyrone and Donegal, it having been found inconvenient bringing people from remote parts'.

Boxty in the pan, resting on the 'crow' (three horseshoes brazed together in the shape of a shamrock).

Boxty Potato

Boxty potato originated in County Derry but is a popular dish throughout Ireland.

Ingredients (Serves 2-4)

30g plain flour
300g peeled raw grated potato
150g butter, melted
Salt and pepper to season
Rapeseed oil for frying

Method

1. Grate potato and drain off starch, add to a bowl. Add butter and flour, season to taste and mix well.

2. In a non-stick pan add some rapeseed oil. When the pan is hot add a thin layer of boxty mix, pressing down with a spoon.

3. Turn when browned at sides, pressing down regularly. Cook for a few minutes on each side until browned and cooked through.

Corned Beef and Cabbage

Ingredients (Serves 8-10)

The Beef

2kg beef brisket joint, trimmed of fat
1 large carrot, peeled and roughly chopped
3 celery stalks, washed and roughly chopped
1 leek, washed and chopped
1 large green cabbage, quartered

Pickling Spices & Brine

1 tbsp whole mustard seeds (brown/yellow)
1 tbsp coriander seeds
1 tbsp red pepper flakes
1 tbsp whole black peppercorns
7 whole cardamom pods
6 large bay leaves, crumbled
2 tsp ground ginger
5 star anise
1 tbsp whole cloves
200g rock salt (optional 5 tsp pink salt)
200g brown sugar
2 glasses white wine
2 litres cold water

Method

1. Dry fry the mustard seeds, coriander seeds, red pepper flakes, cloves, peppercorns, star anise and cardamom pods in a frying pan on high heat until fragrant and you can hear the mustard seeds start to pop.

2. Remove from heat and use a pestle and mortar to crush the spices a little. Add to a bowl and stir in the crumbled bay leaves and ground ginger.

3. Add the fried spice mix to 2 litres of water in a large pot or bowl, along with the rock salt, pink salt (if used), brown sugar and wine.

4. Place the beef into the brine. You can also cure this in a large freezer bag or marinating bag (vacuum pack).

5. Keep sealed in the refrigerator, turning the beef occasionally, for up to 7 days.

6. After the corned beef has been cured in the brine, place it, including the marinating brine, with spices in a large saucepan.

7. Double the total volume with cold water and bring to the boil. Simmer for 2½-3½ hours skimming occasionally.

8. Boil the remaining chopped vegetables until cooked.

9. Pick out the corned beef and allow to rest before slicing.

10. For that added richness, reduce some beef gravy by simmering with a little pickling spices. Serve with the boiled vegetables, boxty potato and spiced gravy.

Lobster fishermen, Giant's
Causeway, County Antrim, 1903.

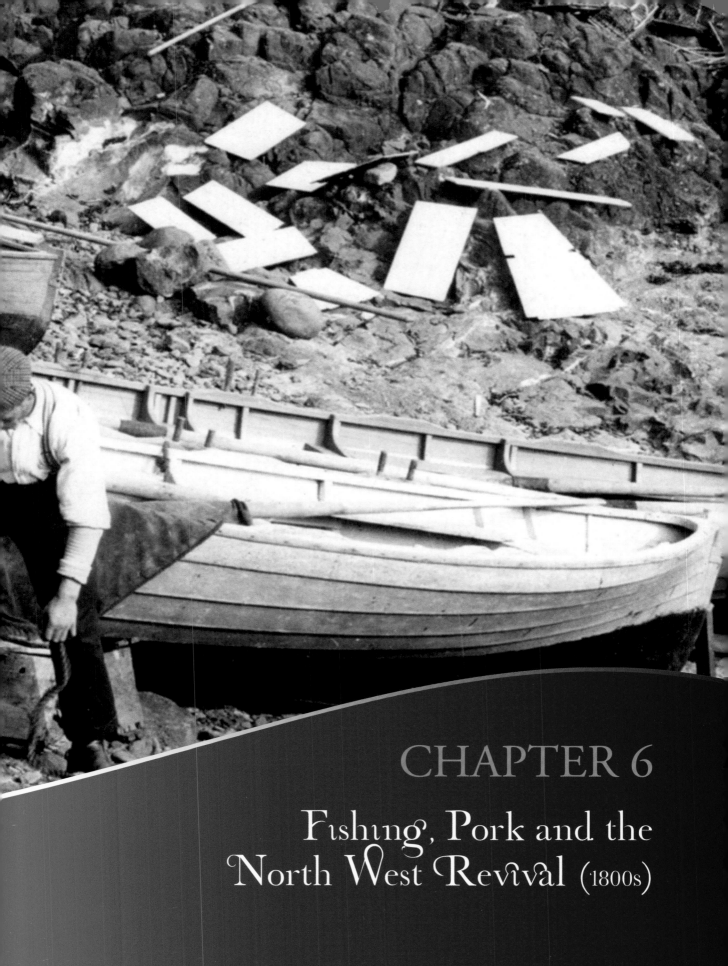

CHAPTER 6

Fishing, Pork and the North West Revival (1800s)

As the 18th century drew to a close, Derry began to enjoy considerable success as both a port and a market town; the population of the city had risen to 11,000 from under 3,000 by 1706. The physical cityscape had started to expand, too. It now took in the Bogside, and new Georgian developments were built along the Strand and in the Waterside. Key to this was a steady influx of new settlers from Donegal. Linen production and shirt making would become huge industries in the city during the 1800s, as, for a shorter period, would shipbuilding. Agriculture, however, was integral to the North West's success. New flour mills, breweries, and distilleries were established, while many skilled culinary artisans, such as butchers, fishmongers, bakers and chefs, set up shop in the city.

One particular success was Derry's fishing industry. For centuries, the Foyle's salmon stocks had been the envy of Europe. But in the early 1800s, with the advent of new processing techniques, a very healthy export business grew up. Because of the huge value of the fishing industry, rights to the Foyle had always been jealously guarded. In the 16th century, Irish chieftains such as Rory O'Donnell (Earl of Tyrconnell), Hugh O'Neill (Earl of Tyrone), Donal O'Carolan (Earl of Clonleigh), together with the Clan MacDermott and the O'Cahans, fought hard to defend the river. But with the Flight of the Earls in the early 17th century, the City of London took ownership of the Foyle.

At the end of the 18th century, a large icehouse was built at Victoria Road to store and process the huge catches of Atlantic salmon which were being taken from the Foyle and its tributaries. Ice for the plant was initially gathered from marshes at nearby Prehen, using picks or ice grips, and pushed down a chute into the icehouse. Such was the demand, however, that ice was then imported from Norway.

Some of the tools used in the process are still on display at the Loughs Agency Historical Centre on Victoria Road in Derry.

The Loughs Agency and Riverwatch Aquarium, Victoria Road, Derry.

The Loughs Agency is responsible for the promotion and development of Lough Foyle and Carlingford Lough for commercial and recreational purposes in respect of marine tourism, fishery and aquaculture matters.

The new facility did not just cater for the Foyle, however. Salmon were brought in to the Derry processing facility from major Donegal fishing ports such as Killybegs and Burtonport. The fish were then ice-packed and exported to London and other British ports. There was a good market for the food in Ireland, too. The salmon (and other goods) would have been transported along the Foyle into the Strabane Canal, via a convoy of barges known as 'The Strabane Fleet'.

Controversially, during the Great Famine of the 1840s, The Irish Society, which controlled the rights to the river on behalf of the City of London, refused to release any salmon to the local inhabitants and instead shipped them to London. Nowadays, most salmon nets have been removed from the Foyle, as the river's stocks have dwindled considerably.

While Derry was enjoying its salmon boom, Inishowen was doing equally well with its herring trade. At one stage there were so many boats on Lough Swilly that, it was recorded, you could walk across them to Rathmullan from the Inishowen coast, a distance of five miles, without touching water.

Fish curing was practised all along the northwest coast in places like Malin Head, Inishtrahull, Moville, Greencastle, Inch Island, Buncrana, Culdaff, Tremone and Lough Foyle. The gutting and curing would have been traditionally carried out by women. The fish were sold at various markets across the region – in Carndonagh, Buncrana, Ramelton, Letterkenny, Portrush and Derry. Some of the fish were exported to Scotland and England, while thousands of barrels of salted herrings were sent to the West Indies and the sugar plantations.

Arthur Young, in Jim Mac Laughlin's book *Donegal: The Making of a Northern County* (2007), had this to say about herring fishing at Inch Island in the 1770s:

Inch is a prodigiously fine extensive island, all high lands, with cultivation spreading over it, and little clusters of cabins with groups of wood; the water

Fishing vessels at Killybegs, County Donegal.

is of a great depth; and a safe harbour for any number of ships. Here is a great resort of vessels for the herring fishing; it begins in October and ends about Christmas. Last year, 500 boats were employed on it; the farmers and coast inhabitants build them and send them out or fish on their own account.

In a middling year each boat will take 6,000 herrings a night. During the season [they fish] six times a week; the price on average is 4 shillings and 2 pence per 1,000 fish from the water. Home consumption takes the most, and the shipping, which lies here for the purpose, the rest … There were that year fish enough in the loch for all the boats in Europe. They swarmed so that a boat went out at 7.00 in the evening, returned at 11.00 full and went out on a second trip. The fellows said it was difficult to row through them, and every winter the [catch] has been great.

In 1776, according to historian Brian Mitchell, shipping magnate Robert Alexander built a salting house on Inch Island capable of curing 100,000 herring a day. The previous year, according to records, Alexander had used one of his transatlantic passenger ships to ferry 1,750 barrels of herring to the West Indies.

Whaling off Greenland

In 1785, a new company was established in Derry to hunt whales off the coast of Greenland. A 400-ton ship was bought and fitted out at the cost of £6,000, but historian Brian Mitchell reports that the initiative was not a success.

Derry Quay, River Foyle.

'Homeward-Bound Salmon'. (Courtesy John R Moore, Irish wildlife and sporting artist.)

Windy City

While Derry generally prospered in the early 1800s, there was occasional disaster lurking in the wings. In January 1839, a deadly hurricane hit the western coast of Ireland, destroying farms, obliterating herds of animals and wrecking fishing fleets. Haystacks and animal fodder were decimated, leading to starvation among livestock that survived the storm. The event, which also left thousands of people homeless, would become known as 'The Night of the Big Wind' (*Oíche na Gaoithe Móire*).

Fillet of Wild Salmon with Boxty Crust, Sloke, Cockle and Willick Sauce

For centuries, the great waterway system of the Foyle has been a gateway for famine ships, travelling monks, armies and the export of many foods produced locally to other worlds. Wild Atlantic salmon have been the jewel in the Foyle's crown and it was known to be the best salmon river in Europe at one time. The people in the coastal areas of Inishowen helped survive during famine times by eating sloke and willicks (periwinkles) and the many other bounties of the sea.

Ingredients (Serves 4)

The Salmon, Sloke, Cockles and Willicks
170g salmon fillet per person
100g butter, diced
300g willicks (periwinkles) and cockles, washed 3 times in cold water (may also use mussels)
75ml dry white wine
200g shallots, diced
2 cloves of puréed garlic
a bunch of finely chopped chives
beurre manié (equal quantities of butter and flour rubbed together to form a paste)
500g sloke (or shredded cabbage), steeped in cold water
100g bacon fat or dripping
a drop of cream
salt and pepper to season
Broighter Gold rapeseed oil for frying

Method
For the Sloke (Sea Spinach)
1. Simmer in water for 3 hours, drain, pat dry and leave aside.
2. When finishing, sauté in bacon fat, butter, puréed garlic and shallots and season to taste.

For the Cockles and Willicks (Periwinkles)
1. In a heavy-based pan, sweat the shallots adding the puréed garlic and white wine, reduce by half by simmering.
2. Add cockles and willicks and cook for 4-5 minutes stirring until the cockles open.
3. Pass through a fine sieve retaining the cockles, willicks and the cooking liquor.
4. Pick out the willicks with a pin, leave aside.
5. Heat the liquid before serving, adding the cream and beurre manié.
6. Simmer, adding the diced cold butter and whisking continually.
7. Transfer the cockles and willicks back into the sauce and the chopped chives.
8. Serve on and around the salmon.

For the Salmon
1. Season the salmon fillets with salt and pepper.
2. Add some rapeseed oil to a frying pan.
3. Put on high heat and when oil is smoking place the salmon fillets into the pan.
4. Colour slightly and turn on both sides. Cook until slightly pink inside.
5. To finish, place salmon on top of sloke and then boxty on top of salmon.

Martin's Island

One of the North West's most famous anglers is Deputy First Minister Martin McGuinness. He also loves to turn his hand to cooking, as is evidenced by this story he recounts about a day out on Lough Mask:

When I and five friends arrived at the shore of Lough Mask in County Mayo for the first of two days fly-fishing, the surface of the water was as flat as a pane of glass. After many fishless hours we called it a day. Tomorrow, we prayed, would hopefully be better.

It was certainly different; the pane of glass had turned into what resembled a raging ocean. All six of us aired our unease at the conditions and the prospect of losing a day's fishing. Our collective decision saw us venture forth on the water.

It very soon became clear that fishing from our two boats in such conditions was proving difficult. We then decided to make our way to one of the many small islands which populate Lough Mask. There we began fishing from the shore, this time with considerably more success than the previous day. By lunchtime we had caught quite a number of very fine trout with at least six of them between one and two pounds in weight.

Preparation being everything, I had included in my bag of fly-fishing tricks one stone of potatoes, a large bag of mushrooms, salt, pepper, butter and a roll of tinfoil purchased earlier in Ballinrobe. Aided by my fishing companion, Terry Crossan, and a sizable quantity of broken twigs, we soon had a fire on the go. The potatoes were washed and wrapped in the tinfoil then set onto the dying embers, followed twenty minutes later by gutted and washed trout and ten minutes later by the mushrooms.

What followed was a feast of uncomplicated culinary delight. All hands quickly downed their fly rods and with the only addition being a sprinkling of salt and pepper and butter for the spuds, we ate our meal. *Delicious!* declared all with pride that they had successfully supplied the most key ingredient – the freshest of fresh Lough Mask trout.

Later in Ballinrobe we learned to our amazement that the island we fished and ate so grandly on was – believe it or not – 'Martin's Island'.

Baked Trout with Potatoes and Carrots

A recipe by Martin McGuinness,
Deputy First Minister

Ingredients

4 cleaned brown trout
100g butter
a good bunch of fresh fennel or dill
1 lemon, sliced
450g potatoes
225g carrots, sliced
salt and black pepper to season

Brown trout from Lough Mask, caught by angler
Maurice McDevitt.

Deputy First Minister Martin McGuinness, an avid
fly-fisherman, was kind enough to give me his
recipe for brown trout.
Below: The beautiful Lough Mask.

Method

1. Preheat the oven to 200C/Gas 6.

2. Place each trout on a piece of buttered tin foil large enough to allow for wrapping.

3. Place a knob of butter and sprigs of fennel/dill inside each fish. Sprinkle with salt and pepper.

4. Wrap whole fennel/dill sprigs around each fish.

5. Top with slices of lemon and seal the foil to form a loose parcel.

6. Put the potatoes in buttered foil, top with a knob of butter and seal.

7. Prepare the carrots in the same way.

8. Cook all the parcels in the oven for 20-30 minutes.

9. The vegetables may take longer than the fish so they should be put in the oven some 5-10 minutes before the fish.

Cured and Smoked Herrings on Toasted Oaten Bread with Gooseberry Preserve

In this recipe, sustainable local mackerel can also be used in place of herrings.

Ingredients (Serves 8)

Cured Herrings

4 whole herrings, cleaned, de-scaled and filleted
2 tbsp sea salt (rock salt)
4 bay leaves
1 small onion, peeled and sliced
1 tsp pickling spice
3 star anise
1 fennel bulb, chopped finely
4 tbsp white wine
300ml water

Smoked Herrings

8 cold smoked herring fillets
Melted butter for glazing

Method
For the Cured Herrings

1. Place the herrings in a deep tray. Rub with salt and pickling spice. Top with bay leaves, onion and chopped fennel.

2. Pour over the wine and water, enough just to cover the fish and marinade/cure for a minimum of 4 hours up to 2 days to maximise the flavour.

3. Grill or bake with some of the curing liquor for 15 minutes at 150C/Gas 2.

4. Serve hot or allow to cool in the liquor.

For the Smoked Herrings

1. Brush the herrings with melted butter.

2. Griddle or bake them until cooked.

3. Serve with oaten bread and gooseberry preserve.

Gooseberry Preserve

Gooseberries have grown wild in the North West of Ireland for centuries and were used mostly for jams and preserves like chutney. They go well with the herrings in this dish as they are naturally tart in flavour complementing this oily fish.

Ingredients

1kg gooseberries, thoroughly washed
200g sweet apples, cored and chopped
200g white sugar
4 tbsp distilled vinegar or white wine
1 clove of chopped garlic
2 star anise
2 tbsp pink peppercorns
1 white onion, finely chopped
1 fennel bulb, finely chopped
1 small sprig of thyme
2 bay leaves
½ tsp salt
1 litre water

Method
For the Gooseberry Preserve

1. Place all the ingredients, apart from the gooseberries, in a copper saucepan.

2. Bring to the boil slowly, stirring well, lower the heat and simmer for 10 minutes.

3. Add the gooseberries, adding more liquid if required.

4. Reduce by simmering until the mixture has thickened. Pour the preserve into sterilised jars.

Emmett demonstrates how herrings were traditionally smoked, hung from a pole across the top of an open hearth.

An Export Economy

Derry's success in the provisions trade grew rapidly at the end of the 18th and the start of the 19th centuries. Brian Mitchell explains, in his publication *The Making of Derry* (1992), that this was linked to the city's booming linen export market. In 1822, 4.5 million yards of linen were sent to Britain, along with 4,000 hundredweight of yarn and 21,000 hundredweight of flax. But the city also exported thousands of barrels of beef, bacon, ham, butter, pork, oats and oatmeal.

Bigger's Pork Stores on Foyle Street were one of the largest and best-known processors in the city.

Workers rolling and packing bacon in one of the city's many pork stores which became one of the largest employers of male labour in the North West, particularly after the closure of the shipworks. The bacon was for local consumption and was also exported worldwide via the city's docks.

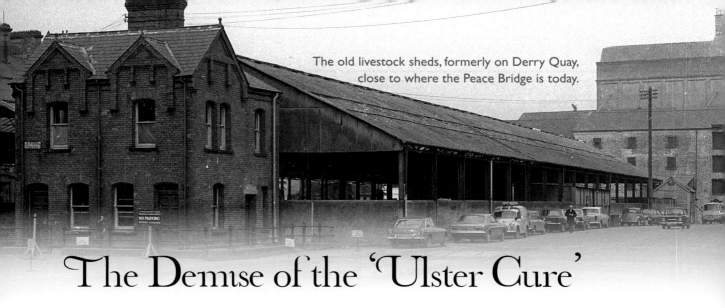

The old livestock sheds, formerly on Derry Quay, close to where the Peace Bridge is today.

The Demise of the 'Ulster Cure'

The history of Derry's pork industry – and the huge contribution it made to the city and the North – is wonderfully recorded in RJ Stewart's thesis: 'A Pig Abattoir and Factory for Londonderry, N. Ireland, June 1968'. In it, he examines how the growth of 'Wiltshire Cure' bacon, gradually supplanted the 'Ulster Cure' method of treating pig-meat.

Stewart makes the case for the development of a new abattoir and factory in Derry to revive the Ulster Cure. He writes: 'Before the last war [WWII], 90% of bacon production was in the form of the traditional Ulster Cure with Wiltshire Cure accounting for the remainder. Now [1968] practically the reverse is true.'

Nonetheless, the number of pigs slaughtered in the North doubled between 1939 and 1965, with exports totalling 75,000 tons in 1966 – 87% of NI's total pig output.

Stewart reports that William Grant & Co (who still operate at Culmore outside Derry) were at the time a 'non-killing curer', produc-

ing about 70% Wiltshire bacon, the remainder in the form of the traditional Ulster Cure.

Grant's, who were established in 1916, had the capacity to process about 900 carcasses a week at the time, with a staff of 30. The company, Stewart reveals, had won a number of Gold Medals for their hams at the International Dairy Show in Edinburgh, 1928.

Trotters and Stout

In Derry, pigs have been reared and exported since the 1700s. In the 19th and 20th centuries, Bigger's, a very popular local Pork Store, sold all cuts, including the feet and the scratchings. There were many eating-houses and takeaways in Derry which sold the cooked trotters, and they were often eaten in the city's numerous bars accompanied by a pint of stout.

Braised Belly of Tamworth Pig, Stuffed Pork Fillet with Black Pudding, Boxty Potato, Wild Bilberry and Crab Apple Jelly

Ingredients (Serves 4-6)

Braised Pork Belly
1½kg Tamworth pork belly, boned and skinned
sea salt and black pepper
Broighter Gold rapeseed oil for frying
1 large carrot, peeled roughly chopped
1 onion, peeled and chopped
1 leek white, chopped
rosemary sprigs
thyme sprigs
2 bay leaves
1 tbsp honey
chilled diced butter
250ml dry white wine
750ml veal or beef jus

Stuffed Pork Fillet
1kg Tamworth pork fillet
salt and pepper to season
250g Tamworth streaky bacon
150g savoy cabbage leaves, blanched and refreshed
1 medium grated carrot
2 tinfoil sheets to roll pork fillet
200g Tamworth black pudding
oil for frying

Wild Bilberry and Crab Apple Jelly
500g wild bilberries or blueberries
500g crab apples
1 litre water
1 lemon rind and 1 tbsp lemon juice
1 orange rind and juice of 1 orange
1 star anise and 2 cloves to flavour
chopped mint leaves
300g sugar

Method

For the Braised Pork Belly
1. Trim pork evenly, rub all over with salt and pepper.
2. In a heavy-based pan add oil, fry pork on both sides and add to a deep roasting tray.
3. Fry vegetables until coloured, drain oil, add vegetables to roasting tray. Add herbs.
4. Deglaze pan with wine and stock, add to roasting tray.
5. Braise in oven for 3½ to 4 hours, turning occasionally, until tender.
6. When still hot, remove pork and place on baking tray, place another tray on top and weigh down with heavy pans. Chill for 4-6 hours.
7. Pass stock through a sieve and, in a pot, reduce by half by simmering. To finish, whisk in diced chilled butter.
8. Slice belly into 3-4cm squared, brush with honey, pan fry until glazed.

For the Wild Bilberry and Crab Apple Jelly
1. Wash apples and bilberries, roughly chop apples. Add fruit to a deep saucepan with all other ingredients, cover with water and simmer for 15 minutes.
2. Pass through a fine sieve and leave to drain, then reduce for a further 10 minutes to achieve a syrup consistency. Pass through a muslin cloth.
3. Pour into shot glasses when cooled slightly and chill to set.

For the Stuffed Pork Fillet
1. Clean and trim the pork fillet removing the chain and fat.
2. Place the pork fillet lengthways on a chopping board, slice inwards along the fillet to form an escalope shape, being careful not to slice straight through. Cover the fillet with clingfilm and baton out flat.
3. Lay the fillet flat on two sheets of seasoned tinfoil.
4. Layer first with streaky bacon then blanched cabbage leaves and finally with grated carrot, season with salt and pepper. Roll as tightly as possible in tinfoil, turning ends as you go.
5. Place on tray and roast in oven for 40 minutes at 180C/ Gas 4 and leave to rest.

For the Black Pudding
1. Slice black pudding into 1cm slices.
2. Panfry until coloured on both sides, 1-3 minutes. Serve with boxty potato, carrots and turnips.

This dish is a celebration of the pig which was often fattened in Ireland for slaughter at important occasions such as harvest time in earlier years. The Tamworth breed is used here as it is the closest to the Irish pig but any rare breed pork can be used. Pigs have been bred in Ireland for their meat for centuries and all parts of the pig were used in cooking. In Derry, pigs were exported using the thriving Port of Londonderry which provided great economic and social benefit to the local breeders and population over many decades. Wild bilberries and crab apples grow abundantly around the North West of Ireland from July through to September.

Crackling Tales

Brandywell man Paddy Roddy has fond memories of Derry's thriving pork industry – not least because it used to sustain him on the long road up to school:

When I was a young boy in the 1950s, my mum would go to the pork stores in Foyle Street for 'parings' and 'trimmings'. She got them for our cousins over the border for boiling with cabbage.

In those days, when you went into a shop to buy bacon it was hanging up in a corded roll for the bacon slicer. The pork store would cut off the uneven bits before they sold the roll of bacon to the shops. They then put all they had cut off in a big tray for selling in the shops as 'parings'.

Derry had no shortage then of pork stores including Bigger's on Foyle Street and Grant's in Bishop Street. (Grant's still have a facility at Culmore on the city's outskirts.)

I used to watch the pigs getting killed in the slaughterhouse. They were shot and then dumped down a chute into a big tank of boiling water, where they then scraped all the hair off the skin. There was a house near the slaughterhouse at the Little Diamond where black puddings were made from the pigs' blood. And sometimes on our way to school, my mates and I would circumvent their homemade security system and feast on warm black puddings on our way up Rosemount Hill.

Support Your Local Butcher

I source my cruibins at one of the many excellent local butchers in the North West. Indeed, I source all my meat through the likes of Gallagher's butchers in William Street in Derry City centre or Paul's Butchers on the Culmore Road on the edge of the city.

Gallagher's is a traditional butchers with a lifetime of experienced staff and has been situated in William Street for over 50 years whilst Paul's Butchers is a more recent establishment, responsible for something of an artisan butcher's revival in recent years. He offers speciality dishes and finished meats as well as complete meals and side dishes. Whilst supermarkets offer a huge selection of meats, often sourced locally and just as fresh, I'm a firm believer in supporting local indigenous businesses. In my experience, the knowledge and expertise of the independent master butchers gets me the finest cuts, supported by their assurance of provenance and very accurate cooking instructions. So get out there and support your local butcher!

The Black Stuff

Brewed in Ireland since 1759, Arthur Guinness's 'porter' (later stout) was a popular drink in the pubs of Derry and Donegal throughout the 1800s and 1900s. Almost a soup in its own right, the working class of the North West consumed unquantifiable barrels of the black stuff in its various varieties over the decades.

Guinness is now widely used throughout the world in a variety of dishes from the ever popular beef and Guinness pie or stew, to Guinness chocolate truffles and the simple Guinness and oysters (or mussels). Check out the Guinness Storehouse site for more recipes with the black stuff (www.guinness-storehouse.com).

The perfect accompaniment to my modern interpretation of cruibins – a pint (or half) of creamy Guinness complements the slightly salty taste of the pork (as can be testified to by the many 'Guinness men' who swear on the simple but mouth-watering combination of salted peanuts and Guinness).

Traditionally, cruibins were plain boiled and eaten au naturel – but in my interpretation they are stuffed with a French-style chicken mousse with wild mushrooms.

The cruibins are then sliced, almost like a terrine, and eaten with a thick bread.

Above: The first bulk delivery of Guinness to Neal Carlin's wine and spirits wholesalers on Cross Street, Derry, in the 1950s. Right: A large billboard for Guinness at the city end of Derry's Craigavon Bridge in the 1920s.

> *'My number one choice would be Guinness.*
> *My number two choice would be Guinness.*
> *My number three choice would have to be Guinness.'*
>
> Actor Peter O'Toole
> on his favourite Irish 'food'.

Crubins With Stout

Ingredients (Serves 4)

The Trotters
4 pigs' trotters (boned out, hairs removed, skin on by your butcher)
2 carrots, peeled and chopped
½ stalk celery, roughly chopped
½ onion, roughly chopped
250ml of dry white wine
300ml beef stock
sprig of thyme
1 bay leaf
salt and pepper to season
Broighter Gold rapeseed oil for frying

The Filling
30g wild mushrooms, morels or chanterelles, cleaned and chopped
1 small onion, diced
300g chicken mousse (minced chicken, an egg white, cream)
pinch of chopped fresh thyme
butter for frying
salt and pepper to season

Method
For the Trotters
1. Soak the trotters in water for 24 hours, drain and pat dry. Singe/scrape off any remaining hairs, particularly around the toes.
2. In a heavy-based roasting tray fry the vegetables. Add the trotters, skin side down, and fry, shaking the tray to prevent them from sticking.
3. Add the wine and reduce by half by simmering.
4. Add the stock, sprig of fresh thyme and bay leaf.
5. Bring to the boil, cover and cook in the oven at 220C/Gas 7 for 3 hours, checking occasionally.
6. Remove and allow to cool. The trotters should be an oak-brown colour when cooked.

For the Filling (Chicken Mousse)
1. Sweat the mushrooms and onion without colour, season well and cool.
2. When the mixture is cool, fold egg white and a drop of cream into the chicken mince to bind.
3. Add the chopped thyme, adjust the seasoning.

Stuffing the Trotters
1. Cut large squares of tinfoil and clingfilm big enough to wrap and seal the trotters.
2. Place the whole trotter, skin side down, on the sheets of foil and film.
3. Pick out the pieces of fat in the trotter, fill the trotters with the mousse and roll in clingfilm and tinfoil to reform its original shape.
4. Twist at either end to secure. Place in fridge for 15 minutes to set.
5. Poach the trotters in boiling water for 15 minutes. Unwrap the trotters and serve with a pint of stout. (Can also be served cold as an appetiser.)

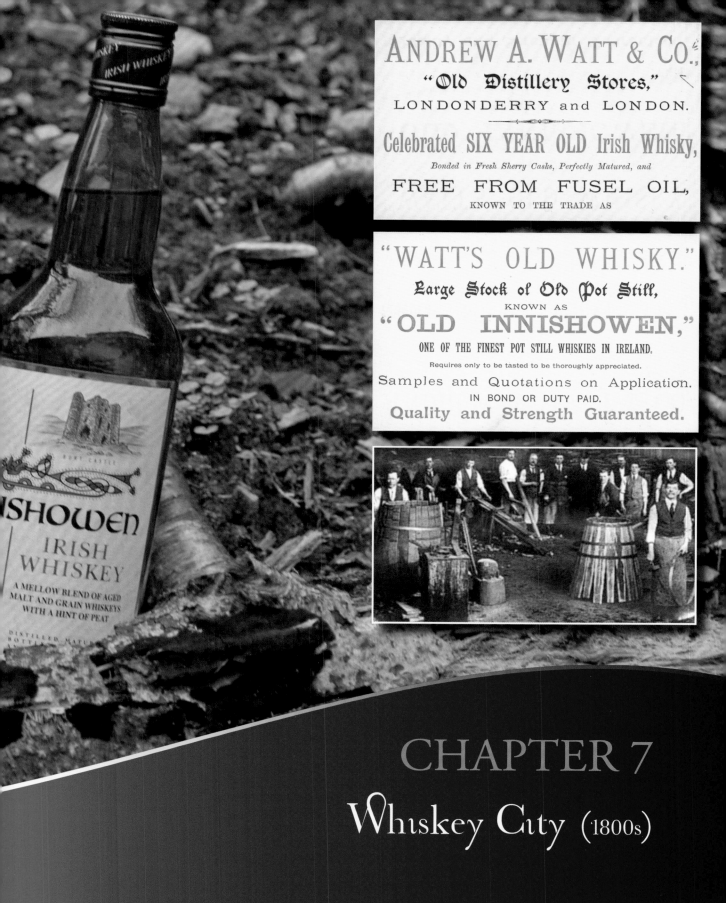

ANDREW A. WATT & CO.,
"Old Distillery Stores,"
LONDONDERRY and LONDON.

Celebrated SIX YEAR OLD Irish Whisky,
Bonded in Fresh Sherry Casks, Perfectly Matured, and
FREE FROM FUSEL OIL,
KNOWN TO THE TRADE AS

"WATT'S OLD WHISKY."
Large Stock of Old Pot Still,
KNOWN AS
"OLD INNISHOWEN,"
ONE OF THE FINEST POT STILL WHISKIES IN IRELAND.
Requires only to be tasted to be thoroughly appreciated.
Samples and Quotations on Application.
IN BOND OR DUTY PAID.
Quality and Strength Guaranteed.

CHAPTER 7
Whiskey City (1800s)

The early 19th century was a boom time for Irish arable farmers, so much so that the country became known as 'the granary of Britain'. Oats, wheat and barley were particularly strong crops, both for home consumption and for export. And because of the huge trade in cereal, Derry was acquiring an international reputation as a major port.

With a healthy surplus of grain in its coffers, the city, and its Inishowen hinterland, began acquiring fame for another 'home-grown', and illicit, product: poteen. Indeed, the revenue commissioners would eventually identify the North West as the centre of the bootlegging trade. Poteen is a spirit of between 60% and 90% proof, commonly made from potatoes or cereal and distilled in a small pot (*poitín* – little pot). One of the strongest alcoholic beverages in the world, it is also known as *uisce beatha* (water of life) or just *uisce* (water). It was outlawed during the 17th century but was still produced throughout Inishowen and sold openly at Derry markets.

Donegal, indeed, was at the forefront of this industry in the early 19th century, producing up to a third of Ireland's poteen, until new legislation was introduced that favoured legal distilleries throughout Ireland. The historian Sean Beattie records that, around 1780–1820, there was a 'massive' distilling operation in Inishowen. Revenue officials estimated there were more than 800 stills in operation, with up to half the homes in the peninsula involved at some level.

The tax inspector Aeneas Coffey blamed the high rents charged by unscrupulous landlords for the proliferation of poteen making in the area, as the local people were living in penury. Coffey also believed landlords were themselves directly involved, anxious to capitalise on the business.

The poteen made in this part of Ireland became known as 'Inishowen' and was of a higher quality than was produced elsewhere in the country. It was often referred to as 'whiskey' (Irish whiskey is spelt with an 'e') and was similar in flavour to Scotch whisky. Urris in Inishowen was famous for making the best-quality poteen of the era. The locals could practise their craft unhindered, as access to the area was difficult and there was no neighbouring police barracks.

James Hewitt, Commissioner of Excise, described Urris as the 'Poteen Republic'. Eventually, a new road had to be constructed through Mamore Gap to allow customs officials, troops and police to undertake raids and root out the illegal stills.

A surviving bottle of Iskaheen poteen.

Poteen from Inishowen would make its way across Ireland via the links established across the Foyle from Moville to Magilligan. Unable to stamp out the poteen-makers, the government was forced to change the law by cutting the duty on legal spirits. This made poteen a much less lucrative business. Indeed, Sean Beattie reports that the price of a gallon of poteen fell by half ('This Destructive Trade', *Donegal Annual*, 1991).

The new legislation favoured distilleries near Derry in particular. The city had ample access to supplies of locally grown barley and clean water necessary to produce malt whiskey of a unique class. And the growing port had the facilities to export the product.

In 1814, William Leathem established a distillery at Bohillion Farm, near Burt, on the Derry to Letterkenny road. It was the only legal distillery in Donegal ever to achieve some measure of success. In order to best the poteen competition, Leathem produced grain whiskey to a very high standard, which matured for at least a year. Burt Distillery sold its whiskey as far afield as Dublin and London, and had an annual production in the 1830s of 40,000 gallons.

Alexander Stewart was the first distiller of whiskey at Pennyburn in Derry, and at its height, his facility was producing 117,000 gallons a year. Ross T Smith had a distillery on Abbey Street in the Bogside, James Robinson a distillery in the Waterside, and by 1836 the combined distilleries of Derry were producing 350,000 gallons of spirits.

Poteen stills seized in Donegal.

A Poteen Song

Oh happy land of careless laughter,
Of heath-clad mountains green
Where fairies dance on the
moonbeams rafter;
Oh, Inishowen – the land of poteen.

Thomas Nesbitt (1891). From *Romantic Donegal: Its Songs, Poetry and Ballads*, Harry Percival Swan, HR Carter Publications, 1964.

Burt Distillery.

But by far the biggest and most famous company of them all came into being in 1839 when Alexander Watt, who originally hailed from Ramelton in Donegal, bought out the Abbey Street distillery. Watt installed the famous Coffey still, which produced a milder flavour, to the delight of a more sophisticated market worldwide.

Despite occasional temperance campaigns, the mid-19th century would become regarded as the golden age of Irish whiskey and Watt's Distillery would be at the forefront, producing two million gallons of spirits a year. Watt's had three major brands: 'Tyrconnell' (the old name for Donegal), 'Favourite' and 'Inishowen'. Up until Prohibition was introduced in America, Tyrconnell was the biggest selling of these.

Watt's whiskey was to become a global phenomenon. Old photographs of the Yankee Baseball Stadium in New York show advertisements for the spirits, and a horse called Tyrconnell, owned by the Watt family, won the Irish Grand National in 1876 – at 100/1 odds! Moreover, the production of whiskey had a very positive effect on the farming sector of this time, as it required 150,000 bushels of grain and malt every year. This equated to 3,600 acres of arable land and created a boom in the local agricultural sector. (For the full story of Derry's whiskey heritage, see Brian Mitchell's *The Making of Derry*.)

The historic Tyrconnell whiskey brand has been kept alive in recent years by Cooley Distillery, as evidenced by their recent Gold Medal awards. Liquor ratings and review aggregator Proof66.com, which assembles expert evaluations of whiskies and other spirits, rates the Tyrconnell 10-Year Madeira Cask Finish among the 20 best whiskies in the world. Tyrconnell Single Malt Sherry Finish was named Best Irish Single Malt at the 2013 World Whisky Awards.

Above: An original pewter bottle (left) from Watt's Distillery and (right) a miniature of Tyrconnell Irish whiskey specially labelled to honour Nobel Peace Prize winner John Hume. Below: William Street entrance to Watt's Distillery.

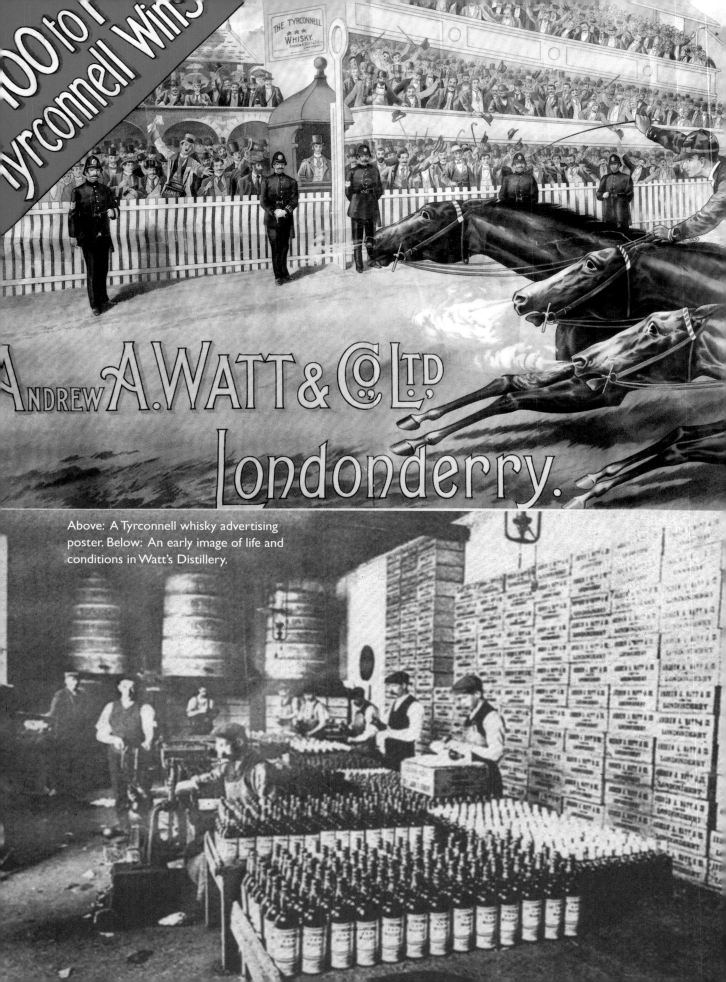

100 to 1
Tyrconnell Wins

THE TYRCONNELL
WHISKY.
ANDREW A. WATT & CO.

ANDREW A. WATT & Cº Lᵀᴰ, Londonderry.

Above: A Tyrconnell whisky advertising poster. Below: An early image of life and conditions in Watt's Distillery.

Tyrconnell Whiskey Cured Salmon

This succulent appetiser/starter is a perfect banquet or party dish and is best marinated for a minimum of 2 days (to a maximum of 4-5 days). This cure takes its origins from the Scandinavian dish Gravlax. Tradition has it that the Vikings may have brought this curing method to Ireland.

Ingredients (Serves 15-20)

1 side (2.5kg) of Atlantic salmon, or large trout, pin-boned by a fishmonger
a large glass of Tyrconnell whiskey
1 large bunch of chopped fresh dill
100g brown sugar
100g coarse sea salt
10g cracked black pepper
30g of yellow mustard seeds
1 lemon, peeled and sliced finely with pith removed

Method

1. Place salmon fillet, skin side down, on a sheet of tinfoil, using enough tinfoil to parcel the salmon later.
2. Rub salt, spices and sugar along the salmon followed by the chopped dill.
3. Place slices of lemon along the length of the salmon.
4. Pour the whiskey along the top, fold over the tinfoil and wrap tightly.
5. Place on a deep tray and place another, smaller tray on top. Weigh it down with heavy pans and place in fridge, turning occasionally, for 2-3 days.
6. Unwrap the salmon, remove the lemon and slice finely like smoked salmon.
7. Serve with pan-fried fadge (potato bread) and horseradish cream.

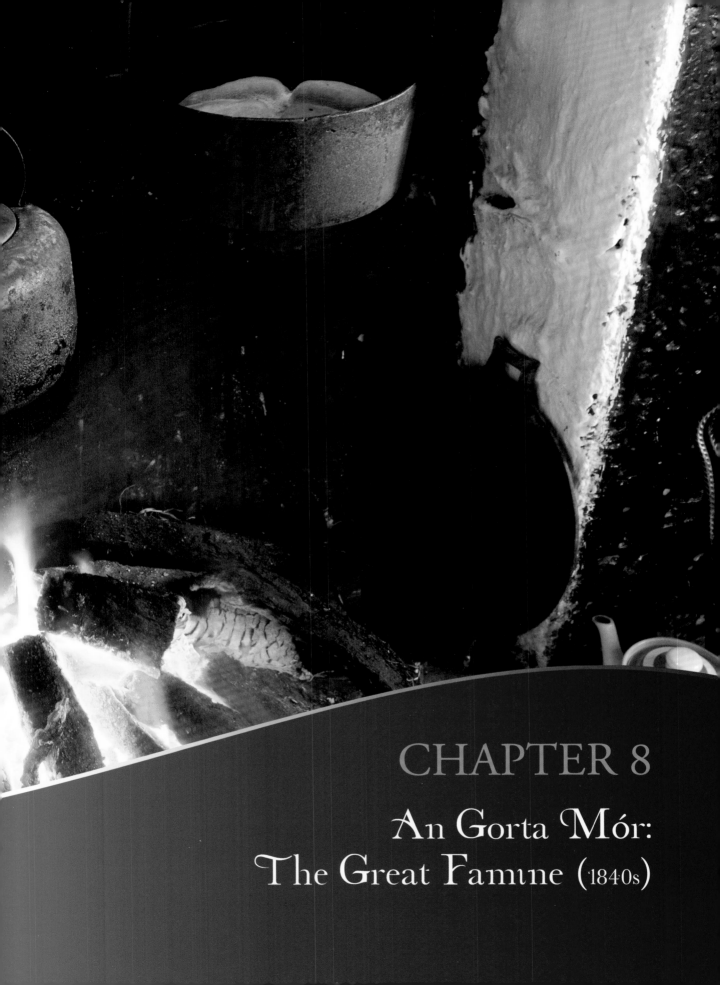

CHAPTER 8

An Gorta Mór:
The Great Famine (1840s)

Mark the Irishman's potato bowl placed on the floor,
the whole family upon their hams around it, devouring a
quantity almost incredible; the beggar seating himself to
it with a welcome; the pig taking his share as readily as the
wife; the cock, hens, turkeys, geese, the cur, the cat and
perhaps the cow – all partaking of the same dish. No man
can often have been a witness to it without being convinced
of the plenty, and I will add the cheerfulness that attends it.

Arthur Young, 1780.

reland's love affair with the potato would turn to tragedy in the 1840s, when a series of blights struck the crop, causing widespread famine across the country. More than a million people starved to death, while a further million emigrated. As we will see, however, Derry's success as a port protected its citizens and, to a certain extent, the people of Donegal, from the worst of the crisis.

At the time of the Great Famine (1845–52), the average man in Ireland consumed 12lbs–14lbs of potatoes a day for most of the year, and his family a percentage of this. Experts believe that the varieties commonly eaten before the famine, including the 'lumper', were much tastier than some bland potatoes available today. The Irishman's gargantuan meals of potatoes and buttermilk provided most of the proteins, calories and minerals he needed and shielded him from diseases such as scurvy, which were common in other countries.

When potatoes were cooked in Ireland, they were often plain boiled with skins intact. At the time of the famine, the preference was for the potatoes to be slightly underdone or 'parcooked'. The terms 'with a bone in them' or 'with the moon in them' were used to describe how the potatoes should be eaten *al dente*. This, of course, meant the potatoes were hard-

er to digest and hence could sustain the people for longer periods of time, especially in times of great hardship or in years of bad yield. The lumper potato was particularly waxy and well suited to this type of cooking: 'We always have our potatoes hard, they stick to our ribs and we can fast longer that way.' Thomas Reid, *Travels in Ireland* (London, 1823).

Popular Derry and Donegal variations on the potato theme included poundies (a version of champ, generally accompanied by a glass of buttermilk), colcannon and fadge (potato bread).

While it took a heavy toll on the North West, the Great Famine (*An Gorta Mór*) did not cause the devastating levels of mortality in Donegal and Derry as it did in areas such as Mayo and Cork. The failure of the potato crop was nothing new to the Donegal people, as they had seen it many times in the early 1800s (1816–19, 1821–22 and 1830–31). Indeed, in some coastal areas the population actually grew, largely because of the abundant fishing grounds nearby. Many were able to survive on a diet of herring, seaweed, limpets and other shellfish. On Inishtrahull Island, nine miles off Malin Head, there was no potato blight at all, so ships from Derry would exchange food with the islanders when leaving and returning to port.

A rural potato market in the early 1900s.

Above: Potatoes were the staple diet of virtually every family in the North West and throughout Ireland for many decades until a series of blights devastated the local supply and caused widespread famine.
Below: An elderly farm worker pauses from her labour to enjoy a meal of potatoes and buttermilk.
(Courtesy WA Green/National Museums NI.)

The Famine Song

Oh, the praties they grow small,
Over here, over here
Oh, the praties they grow small,
And way up in Donegal,
We eat them skins and all,
Over here, over here

Oh, I wish that we were geese,
Night and morn, night and morn.
Oh I wish that we were geese
Till the hour of our release
When we'd live and die in peace,
Stuffing corn, stuffing corn

Oh, they'll grind us into dust,
Over here, over here,
Yes, they'll grind us into dust,
But the Lord in whom we trust
Will return us crumb for crust,
Over here, over here.

Anon, c.1845. Possibly a parody of *The Wonderful
Song of 'Over There'*, published by Atwill in 1844.

'The Potato Diggers' by Paul Henry, 1912,
Aran Islands (Courtesy National Gallery of Ireland)

Bog Butter

Under the Celtic Rundale system of farming, which survived until the 18th century, butter was stored in bogs. Indeed, it is not uncommon, even in the 21st century, for farmers to unearth long forgotten bog-butter boxes in fields across Ireland.

Crops were traditionally sown in the springtime and the cows were sent away to the hills until the harvest was gathered in the autumn. Surplus milk produced in these summer 'booleys' was then made into butter, which was stored in crocks or caskets and kept cool in the bog.

There is a fine example of a bog-butter box on display at the Ulster American Museum outside Omagh.

Abernethy Butter:
handmade and hard to beat

Nestled in the Dromara Hills in County Down, you will find Beechtree Farm where Abernethy Butter is made. Will and Allison Abernethy, who make the butter, are true food heroes and have dedicated themselves to perfecting the art of butter making, using a skill that had been passed down through their family for generations.

Cream is sourced from the farm where the cows are allowed to graze on fresh grass. It is churned by hand into butter and buttermilk and then washed until all the buttermilk is removed and the water is clear.

Pure and additive free, a simple pinch of salt completes the process before it is patted into rolls and wrapped in brown paper.

In terms of flavour and creamy texture, this labour-intensive product stands head and shoulders above so many commercial butter brands.

Throughout the 1840s, farmers in Donegal were able to sustain other foodstuffs, and even at the height of the Great Famine, they were sending oats, butter, eggs, poultry, pork and cattle to local fairs and to Derry markets. In January 1847, when the third year of the blight had devastated crops across Ireland, the *Londonderry Standard* recorded that there were bumper supplies of wheat, oats and butter for the export market. Meanwhile, in Strabane, it was recorded that the quantity of oats and wheat had increased. Butter was also plentiful with Indian meal (corn), bran and turnips in great demand.

The famine did, nonetheless, devastate the poorer population in Inishowen and Donegal. Many of the labourers who lacked the funds to buy food during the famine also lacked the resources to emigrate. The cost of passage to America at the time was equivalent to one year's wages. Moving large families was out of the question; credit was rare and not forthcoming. In some cases, landlords would buy land in exchange for tickets to the New World for a smallholder's family.

Tens of thousands emigrated from Derry port to both America and Australia from 1830 to 1860. By the end of the famine, the Irish made up more than a quarter of the population of cities such as New York, Boston and Philadelphia, while Toronto in Canada was more than 50% Irish. According to Port of Londonderry records, more than 12,000 people left for America alone in 1847 at the height of the famine, the huge bulk of these from Donegal, Tyrone and Derry. Many more travelled to Liverpool, which was the preferred route to the New World.

The poorer population in the North West, who could not afford to travel, either moved to Derry – where they could apply for famine-relief aid or a place in a workhouse – or they stayed put in rural areas and ran the risk of succumbing to starvation or disease.

Tens of thousands emigrated from Derry to America, Canada and Australia throughout the 1800s and early 1900s.

Emigrants from the North West poured onto ships bound for a better life in far-flung lands from the 1700s onwards. But far-off pastures were not always greener. Immigrants were often recruited straight off the ship into a foreign army and thrown directly into conflict, persuaded by promises of regular meals, a small plot of land or basic pay.

The Food That Built a Nation

As America developed over the decades, there emerged a growing demand for a resourceful and hardy workforce to build the nation's infrastructure – houses, roads, bridges, canals, railroads and eventually the skyscrapers which dominate the skyline of the country's biggest city's today. Labourers from the North West arrived in the New World to join thousands of others from around the globe to engage into this back-breaking but much-needed work. Many paid with their lives in some of the most dangerous occupations of the time such as high-steel erection and railroad work. A common expression of the time on the railroads was 'an Irishman is buried under every tie'.

Other Irish immigrants were recruited straight off the ships and fought alongside Americans in the Revolutionary War (1775–83), both sides of the Civil War (1861–65), and numerous conflicts after that.

These early immigrants brought their traditions and culture with them, their old stories, songs and way of life. They also brought their family recipes and culinary heritage. Foods such as colcannon, corned beef, and cabbage and bacon were introduced to the US palate by early Irish settlers and helped fill the bellies of the industrious Irish men who helped build America.

DUFFY'S CUT MASS GRAVE

Nearby is the mass grave of fifty-seven Irish immigrant workers who died in August, 1832, of cholera. They had recently arrived in the United States and were employed by a construction contractor, named Duffy, for the Philadelphia and Columbia Railroad. Prejudice against Irish Catholics contributed to the denial of care to the workers. Their illness and death typified the hazards faced by many 19th century immigrant industrial workers.

PENNSYLVANIA HISTORICAL AND MUSEUM COMMISSION   2004 ®

Traditional Crane Oven

Cooking facilities in the 1840s for the general rural populace were very primitive, usually consisting of just a hearth fire to cook and heat the whole house. The doors of the dwellings were deliberately small to help retain the heat and houses often would have no other source of light because of a tax on windows imposed by landlords (which inspired the phrase 'daylight robbery').

All family life took place around the hearth as reflected in the old Irish saying: *níl aon tinteán mar do thinteán féin* ie 'there's no fireplace like your own fireplace'. A cast-iron pot (aka a Dutch oven) was hung from a chain or pole attached to a wooden or metal beam that stretched above the open fire and was secured at both ends. A crane was also commonly used after the famine and was attached at the side of the hearth. An adjustable crook was then used to hang the pots on and served as a temperature gauge: the lower you held the pot to the flame the hotter it would be. The crane was swung out and away from the fire when the food had been cooked. Hot coals or turf logs were placed on top of the lid of the pot, allowing it to serve as an oven.

The accompanying images of a traditional hearth have been taken by photographer Shane Smith in the unique home of the wonderful Margaret Gallagher. Margaret lives in a 200-year-old cottage near Boho, Belcoo, County Fermanagh. She has no running water or electricity, getting water from the well. Margaret bakes her own bread, cooks in a pot oven, heats water for washing and irons with a box iron filled with fire embers.

91

Indian Meal Bread (Golden Drop)

Ingredients (Makes 1 medium loaf)

500g soda bread flour
500g cornmeal (Indian meal or polenta)
2 tsp baking powder
2 medium eggs, beaten
1 tsp sugar
250ml–500ml buttermilk
1 level tsp salt
30g melted butter

Method

1. Mix flour, cornmeal, baking powder, salt and sugar together in a bowl.
2. Pour in the beaten eggs, milk, and melted butter and mix well to create a stiff dough.
3. Empty onto a lightly floured surface and knead for two minutes. Shape into a round and sprinkle the top with cornmeal.
4. Preheat the oven to 200C/Gas 6. Bake for approximately 40-45 minutes.
5. Leave to cool for five minutes before turning on to a board.
6. Slice and serve warm.

Below: Buttermilk – a key ingredient in traditional baking.

Griddle Soda Bread

Ingredients (Makes 1 medium loaf)

250g soda bread flour
250g plain flour
1 tsp salt
300ml buttermilk
1½ tsp baking powder

Method

1. In a bowl, mix flours, salt and baking powder.
2. Make a well in the centre and stir in enough buttermilk to make a soft dough.
3. Turn onto a floured surface and shape into round.
4. Roll out to 5cm thick and cut a cross on the top of the dough to allow it to rise evenly.
5. Cook on the griddle or in an oven at 200C/Gas 6 for 25-35 minutes.

Homemade Fadge – Potato Bread

Fadge is a famous Derry word for potato bread or fried bread, derived from the term 'a wadge of bread', later becoming fadge when fried.

Ingredients (Serves 4)

500g cooked, mashed potato (well drained)
500g plain flour
150g melted butter
salt and pepper to season
(Dulse Fadge option – ingredients as above with the addition of 200g chopped dulse reconstituted in hot water.)

Method

1. Place cooked mashed potato in a bowl, adding the melted butter.

2. Mix well adding enough flour to form a stiff dry dough. Cup dough to form a ball.

3. On a floured surface, roll the dough out to form 1cm-thick round farls.

4. Cut the potato farls into 4 quarters.

5. Fry on a dry griddle on both sides for 10 minutes until browned.

6. Traditionally served for breakfast with bacon and eggs.

Wheaten Bread

Ingredients (Makes 1 medium loaf)

150g soda bread flour
150g coarse wholemeal flour
100g rolled oats
1 tsp salt
2 tsp baking powder
40g margarine or butter
40g caster sugar
250ml buttermilk

Method

1. Preheat the oven to 180C/Gas 4.

2. Line a baking sheet or loaf tin with baking paper or other non-stick product.

3. Stir the flours, salt, baking powder and sugar together in a bowl.

4. Cut the butter or margarine into cubes and rub into flour mixture.

5. Pour the buttermilk and work the mixture by stirring until you have a consistency that is thick, but not too soft.

6. Shape dough on a lightly floured table and place in a 500g loaf tin or on non-stick tray.

7. Pierce centre with sharp knife and sprinkle lightly with wholemeal flour.

8. Bake in the oven for 30-35 minutes or until a skewer comes out clean after being inserted.

9. Tap the bread on the base; it should sound hollow when cooked.

Scone Bread

This is my mother's scone bread recipe which we ate fresh from the oven with lashings of butter.

Ingredients (Makes 1 large loaf)

500g soda bread flour
500g plain flour
500ml–1000ml buttermilk, enough to bind
2 tsp baking powder
pinch of salt
1 tsp sugar
100g butter, cubed
1 whole egg

Method

1. Preheat oven to 180C/Gas 4.
2. Place the flour, salt and sugar in a bowl. Add the baking powder.
3. Rub in the butter until a sandy texture is formed.
4. Crack in the whole egg and mix well.
5. Add a little buttermilk at a time and mix to form slightly soft dough.
6. Turn out onto floured surface and shape into a round.
7. Place onto baking tray and bake in the oven for 35-45 minutes.
8. Serve hot with butter or jam.

Oaten Bread

Oats appear a great deal in Irish cookery and oaten bread was widely eaten on a daily basis. Bread was traditionally baked in a cast-iron pot with lid – a 'pot oven'. Coals or turf were then placed on top to give radiant heat. Great skill and experience was used in determining the correct coals or turf to be placed on top of the lid to prevent the bread from burning.

Ingredients (Makes 2 medium loaves/1 large)

500g rolled oats
1100g soda bread flour
500ml–1000ml buttermilk
2 tsp baking powder
2 tsp golden syrup
1 tsp salt

Method

1. Place oats, baking powder, flour and salt in a bowl.
2. Add golden syrup and buttermilk gradually.
3. Mix to a stiff dough.
4. Turn out onto a lightly floured surface and knead until smooth, then divide in half.
5. Roll each half into a round, about 6.5 to 7.5cm thick.
6. Place on lightly greased baking sheet.
7. Preheat oven to 200C/Gas 6 and bake for 40 minutes until well risen and golden.
8. Serve warm with lashings of butter.

Janet, an Irish dulse seller, and her seaweed thatched cabin on the Antrim Coast Road. (Courtesy RJ Welch/National Museums NI.)

Hard Times Come Again No More

While we seek mirth and beauty
and music, light and gay,
There are frail forms fainting at the door.
Though their voices are silent,
Their pleading looks will say:
Oh, hard times, hard times, come again no more.

*Verse from a song written in 1854 by Stephen Collins Foster (1826–64),
the son of Derry emigrants and father of American music.*

CHAPTER 9

Fighting The Famine (1840s)

Despite the ravages of the potato blight throughout Ireland in the 1840s, research shows that stocks of grain were not properly deployed. Indeed, while corn and Indian meal were in plentiful supply, more grain left the country than stayed.

When Indian meal first arrived in Ireland, it was deemed 'unpalatable' and was viewed as a cheap substitute to 'real food' like potatoes. Most of the meal had not been properly ground and it had to go through a lengthy, complicated cooking process to ensure the consumer didn't suffer severe bowel complaints. But as time passed, people improvised and learned to bake bread with it so it became more and more popular.

A huge stock of Indian meal was built up without fuss or publicity in 1845, but this was not needed, as in 1845–46 few people perished. This was partly due to the efficacy of relief efforts and to Ireland being able to handle the shortfall. But it was the 1846 blight which was to prove the most devastating and this heralded the true beginning of the Great Irish Famine.

Through my research for this book I learned that there seems to be a sense of collective guilt among the people who survived those tragic times. Most never spoke of it afterwards. They somehow blamed themselves and felt a great shame because of their over-reliance on the potato. But there was also another shame – and a striking contrast. The people in the cities generally survived whereas a lot of the rural communities perished. It is said that the very wealthy even took day tours at the height of the Great Famine from Derry to Moville and Donegal where the famished poor in the rural areas were succumbing each day to starvation.

William Smith-O'Brien, a wealthy landowner from Dromoland Castle, County Clare, who was sympathetic to the plight of the poor, observed in 1846:

> The circumstances which appeared most aggravating was that the people were starving in the midst of plenty, and that every tide carried from the Irish ports corn sufficient for the maintenance of thousands of the Irish people.

Moville in the late 1800s.

Bringing home the spuds, Culdaff, early 1900s. (Courtesy WA Green/ National Museums NI.)

That same year, a coastguard officer, Robert Mann, travelling through County Clare, reported seeing innumerable starving and desperate people. But he also encountered huge convoys of food bound for export: 'We were literally stopped by carts laden with grain, butter, bacon, etc being taken to the vessels loading from the quay. It was a strange anomaly.'

At the time of the famine, the destitute of the North West travelled to coastal areas in search of food and the bounties of the sea. Seaweed was widely used for food and for fertilisation of crops – and even roofing of some dwellings. The seaweed along the coastline of Inishowen and Derry had many health properties which sustained the population during famine times.

In *Donegal: The Making of a Northern County*, Charles McGlinchey reports how locals would have gone to the strand at the time of the spring tide (*rabharta mór*) to gather shore food (*cnuasach*) such as dulse (edible seaweed), shells (*sliogain*) and carrageen (Irish moss, containing the vegetable gelatine agar-agar, excellent for jellies and mousses). Shellfish like Queen Anne scallops and razor clams were also in abundance along Lough Foyle. Sloke, or sea spinach, which was found on rocks, was a vegetable substitute high in iodine and iron.

William McElhinney gathering dulse along the Inishowen coastline.

Dulse is still widely used as a food source in the North West and throughout Ireland. Opal or crimson in colour, and rich in potassium and magnesium, it is normally dried out before being eaten. Dulse is a great food accompaniment used to enhance the flavour of other foods like potatoes, oatcakes or bread. Shell dulse (*creathnach*) is a more highly prized delicacy in the North West and has a lighter flavour than common dulse. This shell dulse normally can be found alongside small mussels on the shorelines of the North West and Inishowen. Picked fresh off the rocks, dulse has always been used by older generations as a form of chewing gum, often used by farm labourers to help them through the working day. I always recall my father eating from bags of dulse while on holidays to the seaside and offering us some.

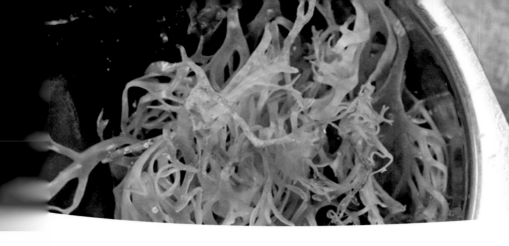

Carrageen Moss and Loganberry Pudding

Carrageen moss (Irish moss) is a seaweed found on the coastal areas of Counties Donegal and Derry. It contains the natural vegetable gelatine agar-agar and is used to make excellent jellies, breads and pastries. It is widely used boiled with milk in Inishowen as a cure for upset stomach. The people of the North West have been using it for generations for desserts such as mousses and blancmange. Loganberries are wild berries that grow along the hedge rows of Derry and Donegal in summer. The taste is similar to the raspberry although sweeter.

Ingredients (Serves 6)

Carrageen Pudding
100g carrageen moss
5 egg yolks
½ fresh vanilla pod (or a few drops of vanilla essence)
150ml cream
2 tbsp of sugar
500ml milk
rind of ½ lemon

Loganberry Coulis
300g loganberries or raspberries
100g sugar
squeeze of lemon Juice
300ml of cold water

Method
For the Loganberry Coulis
1. Place the loganberries with sugar and squeeze of lemon juice in a blender. Slowly add the water and blend until a sauce is achieved. Taste, adding more sugar if required.
2. Pass through a sieve and pour to fill the bottom of a glass or mould.
3. Leave to set in the fridge for 10 minutes before adding the carrageen mixture.

For the Carrageen Pudding
1. Steep the carrageen in hot water for 10 minutes and then drain.
2. Simmer in the milk and cream for 10 minutes with the lemon rind and scraped out vanilla seeds and vanilla pod.
3. In a bowl, whisk the egg yolks and sugar together until pale in colour.
4. Pour the milk and carrageen through a sieve onto the whisked sugar and egg mixture.
5. Whisk and pour back into a saucepan.
6. Slowly heat without boiling, whisking continually until it coats the back of a spoon.
7. Pour into the loganberry moulds and chill to set. Serve with whipped cream or honeycomb ice cream.

Famine Oatcakes

One of the oldest Irish foods, prominent in Derry and Inishowen, oatcakes were eaten with very little else apart from buttermilk and potatoes. Traditionally, after being baked on a griddle or bake stone, the oatcakes would be hardened in front of the fire. Because of the longevity of cakes and bread made with oats, they were often given to people about to set off on a long journey, such as the famine ships and Scotch boats for seasonal work.

Ingredients (Serves 8)

500g flour
500g medium oatmeal or coarse porridge oats
1 tsp salt
150ml water
125g butter

Method

1. Place oatmeal in a bowl, sift in the flour and salt, making a well in the centre.

2. Place the water and butter in a saucepan and bring to almost boiling to melt the butter. Pour into the well.

3. Mix quickly together adding a little more water if necessary to form stiff dough that holds together.

4. Sprinkle with a little extra oatmeal and roll out thinly.

5. Cut into 5cm rounds and place carefully onto a greased baking tray.

6. Preheat oven to 180C/Gas 4. Bake for 20-25 minutes until golden brown or cook on the griddle or bake stone, turning occasionally.

7. Serve with Famine Soup or great with cheese. Can be kept for several weeks stored in an air-tight tin.

Numerous famine ships left Derry over the years and often many of the more frail or younger passengers did not survive the long arduous journey to the New World.

Famine Testimony

In October 1845 came the first potato blight. We had a field of potatoes that year on the back land and in one night they were struck with the blight & both tops & roots were blackened. The damage done in '45 was only partial, that is to say, only a portion of the country was affected & the blight did not strike the plants until the crop was almost matured … On the night of 3 Aug 1846 came the bad potato blight.

I remember driving to Bundoran through County Fermanagh with my sister Bella on 3 Aug, as we went seeing the fine crops of potatoes in the fields. We spent three days in Bundoran & returning found these same crops blackened & useless. The same state of affairs prevailed practically over the whole of Ireland & in consequence 1847 was the famine year. It was felt severely here, but nothing like so much so as in the South & West. Indian corn and meal were introduced for the first time from America, and I remember the poor people coming into the shop & asking to see 'this yellow meal'. They would then take some in their hand, ostensibly to look at it as a novelty, but really to satisfy their hunger with it.

The fever followed the famine and broke out even in the emigrant ships in which the poor people were fleeing to America … The fever was not so rife here as further west and south, but I remember feeling nervous about it when in Enniskillen, for two of our oldest customers there contracted the disease and died. They sold meal & bread, and probably the poor starving people who came to seek for food had brought the infection.

(James Brown, NI Public Records Office, 1904)

Scenes of Old Ireland

Common scenes of old Ireland (c.1900): 1. An old hearth with a teapot hanging by a chain over the open fire. 2. A domestic scene with a mother and daughter spinning. 3. A group of young children on a donkey and cart on their way to the village. 4. Sheep for sale at a local market. 5. An Irish grandmother hard at work on a spinning wheel.

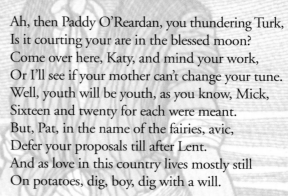

The Potato-Digger's Song

Come, Connal, acushla, turn the clay,
And show the lumpers the light, gossoon!
For we must toil this autumn day,
With Heaven's help, till rise of moon.
Our corn is stacked our hay secure,
Thank God! and nothing, my boy, remains
But to pile the potatoes safe on the flure,
Before the coming November rains.
The peasant's mine is his harvest still,
So now, my lads, let's work with a will.

(Chorus)
Work hand and foot,
Work spade and hand,
Work spade and hand
Through the crumbly mould.
The blessed fruit
That grows at the root
Is the real gold of Ireland.

Och, I wish that Maurice and Mary dear
Were singing beside us this soft day!
Of course they're far better off than here;
But whether they're happier, who can say?
I've heard when it's morn with us, tis night
With them on the far Australian shore.
Well, Heaven be about them with visions bright,
And send them childer and money galore,
With us there's many a mouth to fill,
And so, my boy, let's work with a will.

(Chorus)

Ah, then Paddy O'Reardan, you thundering Turk,
Is it courting your are in the blessed moon?
Come over here, Katy, and mind your work,
Or I'll see if your mother can't change your tune.
Well, youth will be youth, as you know, Mick,
Sixteen and twenty for each were meant.
But, Pat, in the name of the fairies, avic,
Defer your proposals till after Lent.
And as love in this country lives mostly still
On potatoes, dig, boy, dig with a will.

(Chorus)

Down the bridle road the neighbours ride,
Through the light ash shade, by the wheaten
sheaves.
And the children sit on the mountain side,
In the sweet blue smoke of the burning leaves;
As the great sun sets in glory furled,
Faith, it's grand to think, as I watch his face,
If he never sets on the English world,
He never, lad, sets on the Irish race.
In the West, in the South, new Ireland's still,
Grow up in his light; come, work with a will.

(Chorus)

But look! the round moon, yellow as corn,
Comes up from the sea in the deep-blue calm.
It scarcely seems a day since morn;
Well, the heel of the evening to you, ma'am!
God bless the moon! for many a night,
As I restless lay on a troubled bed,
When rent was due, her quieting light
Has flattered with dreams my poor old head.
But see, the basket remains to fill;
Come, girls, be alive; boys, dig with a will.

(Chorus)

The Popular Poets And Poetry of Ireland,
Thomas C Irwin, Richard Nagle, 1887.

Above: The approved diet for inmates of the Derry workhouse in February 1842.
Below: The Derry workhouse.

The Workhouse

One institution, long feared by Ireland's poor, was to become the last refuge for the destitute and hungry during the Great Famine: the workhouse. After the Poor Law was passed in 1834, persons who sought 'relief' were to be granted it, but only through a workhouse setting. Conditions in the bleak buildings were deliberately made as miserable as possible to encourage people to seek work or other means of support for them and their families elsewhere.

The workhouse on Glendermott Road in Derry's Waterside was built in 1840 to house 800 inmates. The building, which ceased functioning as a workhouse in 1947, is now a museum containing many artefacts from the original site.

Museum guide James Coyle has conducted extensive research into what life was like for the workhouse residents: 'Families were split up when they came in. Men were separated

from women, daughters from their mothers and sons from their fathers. If they had allowed them to stay together they would have remained in the workhouse longer. It was the kind of place where they wanted them out as soon as possible. The people slept crammed in rooms on beds of straw infected with lice from farm animals.'

Inmates were given rations of oats and bread or *brochan* (stirabout or porridge), as in most of the workhouses throughout the North West. But the meagre provisions were not always enough to sustain the residents and many still perished. In one section of the Derry workhouse there is still a 19th-century hearse, which was used for transporting dead bodies to the unmarked graves.

Ninety thousand people went into Irish workhouses in 1849, with a further 104,000 entering in 1850.

- Christmas Dinner in Workhouse, 1846 -

Broth,
Stewed Beef,
Soup & Bread,
Coffee,
Fruit,
Bread & Cakes

This was followed in the evening with entertainment as 'some sang and other danced to the scraping of an old fiddle until the sound of the evening bell warned them to return to their dormitories.'

Christmas dinner in the workhouse, 1846.

- MAY - August 1846 -

DINNER DIET

Bread & Sweetmilk - 4 Days
Oxhead Soup - 3 Days

BREAD ALLOWANCE

WORKING MEN:	12oz
WORKING WOMEN:	8oz
CHILDREN ABOVE 13 YEARS:	8oz
OLD, INFIRM, CHILDREN 9-13YEARS:	6oz
CHILDREN 2-9 YEARS:	4oz

Workhouse inmate bread rations, 1846.

MARCH 1847

BREAKFAST:	Flummery 1 Pint ½ Pint Sweetmilk
DINNER:	½lb Bread ½ Pint Sweetmilk
SUPPER:	Flummery 1 Pint ½ Pint Sweetmilk

- JUNE 1848 -

SUNDAY AND THURSDAY
Bread & Soup

MONDAY AND WEDNESDAY
Rice & Milk

TUESDAY & FRIDAY
Stirabout & Milk

SATURDAY
Oatmeal

1845-50
An Gorta Mor
Brachán House
Carndonagh

SAN IONAD SEO A RANNADH MIN
BHUI AR AN OCRACH SA
DROCH SHAOL.
INDIAN MEAL WAS DISTRIBUTED
FROM THIS CENTRE DURING
THE GREAT FAMINE

CHAPTER 10

Famine Heroes (1840s)

The Great Famine would become a watershed in relations between Ireland and England. The London Government's response to the devastation in Ireland was completely inadequate. Sir Charles Trevelyan, who was in charge of the administration of famine relief, lobbied to reduce support for the victims on the grounds that 'the judgement of God sent the calamity to teach the Irish a lesson'. New laws were enacted that forced any tenant farmer applying for relief to sign his land back to the landlord before going through the doors of the workhouse.

The proud Irish refused to ask England – or any other nation – for charity. Nonetheless, they would receive it from a number of staunch supporters in Europe and the New World.

One of the most practical interventions came from the celebrated French chef Alexis Soyer (1810–58), who began campaigning in the British press for support for Ireland. Soyer was subsequently appointed by Parliament to assist in the relief of the famine and he arrived in Dublin in April 1847. His first action was to set up and run the country's first soup kitchen. To this end, he created a special, nutritious 'Famine Soup', which at its height was feeding up to 10,000 people a day in Dublin. Soyer claimed the soup, taken once a day along with oat biscuits, could sustain a healthy man.

Hearing of his efforts, Quakers (Society of Friends) in England and America raised the funds to pay for 'Famine Pots' (huge portable cooking vessels) and the ingredients for Soyer's Famine Soup. Soup kitchens, following the Soyer method, were set up throughout Ireland and organised by the 'Big Houses', ie the wealthy landowners, in each region. It is estimated that the relief effort may have saved up to three million people from starvation and death. The Big Houses, however, were almost exclusively Protestant-owned, and many of the hungry needy were only given soup if they renounced their Catholicism – hence the phrase 'taking the soup'. The soup kitchens were subsequently abolished in 1848 with the introduction of the Workhouse Order, which meant only those with less than a quarter acre of land were entitled to Poor Relief.

Soyer, meanwhile, turned his hand to writing, producing the book *Soyer's Charitable Cookery*, the proceeds of which went to the Irish poor. This book, as you would expect, contains his 'Beef Leg and Bone (Famine Soup)' recipe. The poor of Ireland would not have known the nutritive value of the beef and bones, as Soyer did, given that meat of any kind was a luxury at the time. The recipe (see overleaf) looks to any cook very much like a cross between French onion soup and a beef broth.

THIS IS A FAMINE POT WHICH WAS USED TO FEED UP TO 800 PEOPLE EVERY DAY DURING THE POTATO FAMINE IN IRELAND BETWEEN 1845 - 1848

THE
Modern Housewife
OR
MENAGÈRE.

COMPRISING
NEARLY ONE THOUSAND RECEIPTS
FOR THE ECONOMIC AND JUDICIOUS
PREPARATION OF EVERY MEAL OF THE DAY,
AND THOSE FOR
THE NURSERY AND SICK ROOM;
WITH MINUTE DIRECTIONS FOR FAMILY MANAGEMENT
IN ALL ITS BRANCHES.

Illustrated with Engravings,
INCLUDING THE
MODERN HOUSEWIFE'S UNIQUE KITCHEN, AND MAGIC STOVE.

BY
ALEXIS SOYER,
AUTHOR OF " THE GASTRONOMIC REGENERATOR,"
(REFORM CLUB.)

TWENTIETH THOUSAND.

LONDON
SIMPKIN, MARSHALL, & CO., STATIONERS' HALL COURT;
OLLIVIER, PALL MALL.
1851.

Above: Famine hero Alexis Soyer created many nutritious and economical recipes for the starving and needy in Ireland. Below: The final resting place of Alexis Soyer, Kensal Green Cemetery, London.

To the Memory of
MADAME SOYER.
DIED SEPTEMBER 1ST 1812
AGED 32 YEARS
England gave her birth
Genius Immortality

Also
ALEXIS BENOIT SOYER.
DIED AUGUST 5TH 1858
AGED 48 YEARS

110th THOUSAND

SOYER'S
SHILLING
COOKERY
FOR THE
PEOPLE
G. ROUTLEDGE
LONDON & NEW

ONE SHILLING OR TWENTY FIVE CENTS

TO HER

Alexis Soyer's Famine Soup

Ingredients for Original Recipe from 1847
(Sufficient to feed 1,000 people from a famine pot)

12½lbs leg of beef
100 gallons of water
6¼lbs drippings
100 onions and other vegetables
25lbs each of flour (seconds) and pearl barley
1½lbs brown sugar
9lbs salt

Ingredients for Modern Interpretation
(Serves 6)

1000g beef leg bones
2 litres water or beef stock
100g butter
1 onion, peeled and chopped
200g other vegetables available (turnips/leeks), chopped
100g flour
200g pearl barley
50g brown sugar
Salt to season

Method
1. Melt the butter in heavy-based pot, sweat the onions and other vegetables without adding colour, add sugar and flour and cook until coloured.
2. Add pearl barley and stock.
3. Bring to the boil and simmer for 45 minutes to 1 hour, adjust the seasoning.
4. Serve from the pot with oat cakes.

I like to believe that the shin-beef soup opposite, which my mother used to make a century and a half later, derived from the same great recipe devised by Soyer to combat the famine.

Shin Beef Broth

Ingredient (Serves 6)

500g shin beef bone (with plenty of meat on the bone)
3 carrots, peeled and chopped
2 onions, peeled and chopped
200g soup celery
1 medium leek, chopped
100g pearl barley
100g lentils (optional)
2 litres water or beef stock
salt and pepper to season

Method

1. Sweat off the vegetables in a saucepan, add the shin beef.
2. Add the pearl barley, lentils and water or stock.
3. Bring to the boil and simmer for 2-3 hours, stirring occasionally.
4. Remove the beef shin from the broth and pick the meat off the bone to serve in the soup.
5. Serve with boiled potatoes with their skins on, for that full nutritional meal.

'Spirit of the Earth' by Gary White Deer, commissioned for the Irish Food Heritage Project.

Black '47

The year 1847 would become known as Black '47, the worst year of the Irish Famine. Support came from all over the world, including expats in the US and Australia, the Quakers, and from Irish regiments in India. But it also came from even less likely quarters – including Native Americans.

One major contribution came from the Choctaw tribe, who themselves had suffered great hardship 16 years previously when they had been forced off their land in the south of the country by the federal government and made to move 1,000 miles west to present-day Oklahoma. Thousands of Choctaw died of starvation and exhaustion on this 'Trail of Tears', and they did all they could to prevent the poor in Ireland experiencing similar suffering. In all, they collected $170, which was a huge gesture of humanitarian aid in the 1840s, equating to $20,000 in today's money.

The Native Americans also shipped large amounts of Indian meal to Ireland to help with the famine-relief effort. And the Choctaw sent thousands of blankets, some of which can be seen in photos taken of Irish women post-1850. Indeed, the similarities between the Native American women and Irish women are quite striking.

Below: Irish women in the early 1900s wearing attire similar to Native American women (above) of the same era.

The Choctaw donation was largely forgotten until the late 1980s, when Irish researchers discovered references to it and other small donations from around the world, during preparations for the 150th anniversary of the famine. A great friendship grew up between Derry author Don Mullan and Gary White Deer of the Choctaw Nation. And in 1988, Mullan and a number of other Irish hikers walked the historic Trail of Tears to offer a donation of $20,000 to the Choctaw in return for their gesture 140 years earlier. Then, in 1997, Derry charity campaigner Richard Moore walked the Trail with Mullan and members of the Choctaw Nation to raise £100,000 for the starving poor of Africa.

I met Gary White Deer on a beautiful sunny day in November 2011 on the shores of Lough Swilly, where he talked about the Choctaw-Irish link. White Deer felt that the original 1847 donation was 'a transcendence of the human spirit', as the Choctaw knew nothing of the Irish, only that they were hungry and destitute. In their own teachings, the Native American Nations are taught that feeding someone is the greatest gift you can give – it is extending human life.

Gary White Deer of the Choctaw Nation with Emmett McCourt, Irish Food Heritage Project, overlooking Lough Swilly in 2011.

Below: Gary White Deer has a strong connection with the North West and has painted several community murals including this one in Creggan in the 1990s.

Left: Gary's daughter Janie Willis Zah in traditional dress.

'Trail of Tears' by Gary White Deer, painted in
remembrance of the enforced eviction of the
Choctaw Nation from their homelands in 1831.
This tragic event prompted their assistance to
the Irish during the Great Famine.

Letterkenny market in the early 1900s.

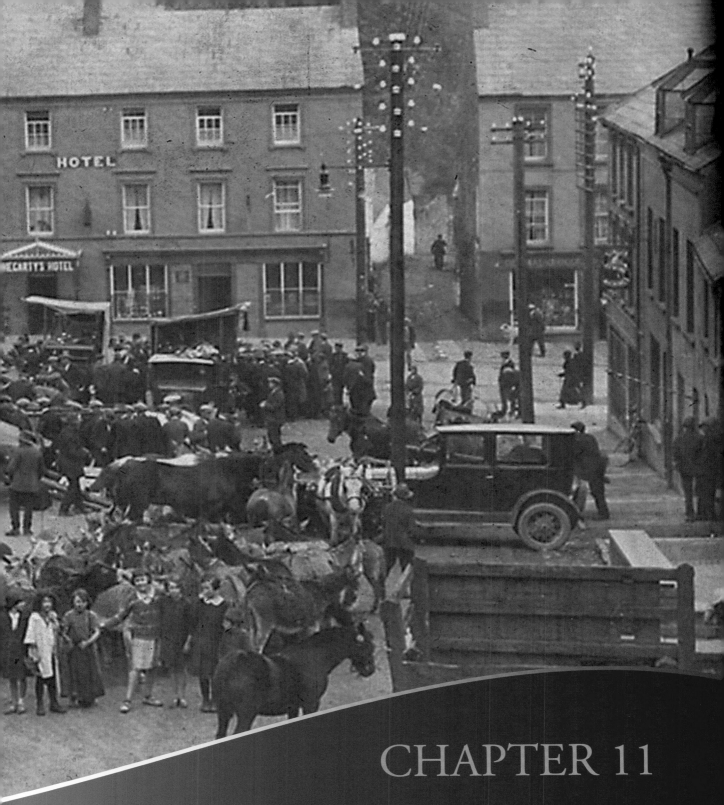

CHAPTER 11
Markets and Fairs (1800s—1900s)

A great riot of nomadic colour this, with swarms of children playing under the caravans or about the openings of the lower tilts, and the buxom, brightly shawled women busy taking silver in exchange for news of dark-advised strangers whom they saw in the upturned palms of laughing country boys and girls.

Richard Hayward on the Puck Fair, 1946.

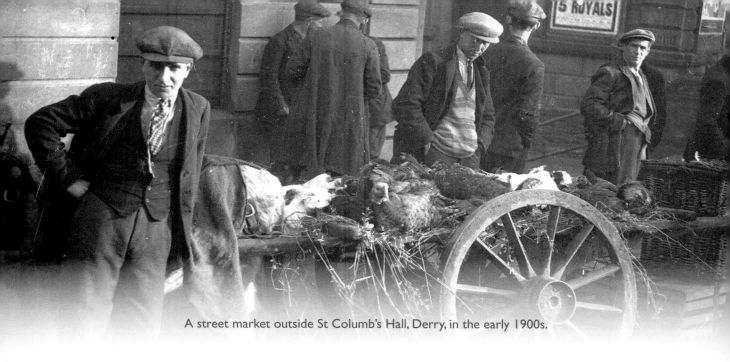

A street market outside St Columb's Hall, Derry, in the early 1900s.

The latter half of the 19th century saw rapid growth in Derry's ship-building and shirt-making sectors. The advent of steamships, as internationally championed by Derry shipbuilder William Coppin, allowed for speedier imports. In North America, expats from the North West fought on both sides of the Civil War, with the Union army sustaining its troops largely on Irish potatoes grown in New England.

Irish butter had also achieved worldwide fame because of the unique salting techniques used in its production. The product had been widely exported since the mid-18th century, and in the late 19th century many visitors arrived to study its manufacture. There was a core regional difference in butter making in Ireland: in the north the whole milk was churned while in the south only the cream was used. In 1877, writer Thomas Baldwin observed that more dairy farmers were using barrel churns, which produced butter more quickly. He also commented that the older 'plunge' churn produced excellent butter but required a lot of time and labour, especially when whole milk was churned.

Buttermilk was a by-product of the production process and in the 19th century, con-sumption of this would have exceeded that of actual milk itself in the North West.

Another industry which enjoyed a renewed surge in the latter half of the 19th century was fishing, according to WP Gaskell in Jim Mac Laughlin's *Donegal: The Making of a Northern County*. Indeed, in 1880, mackerel were in such abundance at Malin Head that you could catch them using 'bags and baskets from the rocks and beach'. Other popular seafood and fish harvested around Inishowen were cod, haddock, halibut, herring, ling, plaice, pollock, sole, turbot, salmon, flatfish, crabs and lobsters.

Markets where fish were sold included Carndonagh, Moville, Buncrana, Ramelton, Letterkenny and Portrush, with Gaskell reporting that more than 600 tons of seafood were exported from the Foyle alone in 1898 in upwards of 8,000 boxes. Inishowen locals would also have traded fish for whisky with their neighbours on nearby Scottish islands such as Islay.

The market was, of course, the centre of agricultural commerce in the North West. Markets would have been held once a week, with a fair once a month. Until the 20th century, city and town dwellers were dependent

A typical market scene in rural Ireland in the early 1900s.

on markets for their supplies and necessities – potatoes, vegetables, fowl, meat, butter and eggs, in addition to fuel and grain. And pedlars then brought items that were not produced locally, for example salt for making and keeping butter, while coopers attended to sell tubs and barrels.

Commenting on the Carndonagh Fair in 1898, a *Derry Journal* reporter wrote: 'Carn fairs are held quarterly and are big days in the lives of the farming community. At these fairs, horses, cattle, sheep and pigs, together with oats, potatoes and other articles of farm produce, as well as butter, eggs, fish and fowl are offered for sale. Servant boys and girls can also, as a rule, be engaged in these markets, but not in such numbers as in Strabane or Letterkenny.'

The fairs and markets instilled a great sense of community among the attendants. Some events lasted for days. Fairs such Magheramore and Ardara in Donegal were famous and the people came from miles to socialise. First, the selling of the livestock took place; food was then cooked and sold; and finally, the festivities took place. Post-lunch events included horse racing, matchmaking and 'courting'.

According to tradition, all sorts of tradesmen brought their wares to the fairs: weavers sold frieze, drugget and linen; coopers sold churns, noggins and firkins. There were also blanket-makers, nailers, ironworkers and tinsmiths. Ireland's travelling community played a major role in the events – they were skilled craftsmen and specialised in metal and tin work (hence 'tinkers') – and to keep the crowds in celebratory form, there were musicians, singers, dancers and, of course, sellers of poteen.

Hiring fairs or 'rabbles' or 'gallops' were also a part of the community's social life in the 19th century. In May and November, men, women and children would offer themselves in public for hire for six-monthly seasonal work on farms. Children as young as seven, from struggling families, were hired out to ensure their parents had fewer mouths to feed. For the townspeople, the fair was a holiday and public entertainment, but for those country people seeking work, it was a time of uncertainty. They hoped for good pay and they knew they would not see their families and homes for six months.

A hiring fair or 'rabble' in Derry's Diamond in the 1920s.

Travellers were an essential element of the traditional Irish market/fair experience.

The Walking People

There are folklore strands that suggest Traveller culture and itinerant lifestyle originated in the potato famine of the mid-1800s although there is no solid evidence to support this. Some scholars suggest that Irish Travellers are descendents of itinerant craftsmen and metal workers known as 'Tinkers' (now considered a derogatory term). Or they may have descended from wandering musicians and storytellers. Other scholars trace Irish Travellers further back in history, even to pre-Celtic times.

It is true to say, however, that many Irish families were dispossessed of their homes during the Cromwellian war in Ireland (1649-53) and at later times, particularly during the potato famine, this may have resulted in families adopting a nomadic lifestyle to increase their chances of survival. They were a resilient and resourceful people and not being tied to the land meant they could forage for food wherever they could find it.

Irish Travellers share their own, distinct language, Gammon or Cant, and refer to themselves as Minceir or Pavees. In Irish they are known as an *lucht siúil*, meaning 'the walking people'.

The following is a variation of a Traveller soup recipe passed down through the generations:

Palhm Mafon skai/Famine Soup recipe
4 oz (½ cup) of beef
2 oz (¼ cup) dripping
2 onions
8 quarts water
8 oz (1 cup) flour
8 oz (1 cup) barley
½ oz (1 tsp) brown sugar
3 oz (⅓ cup) salt

Recipe extracted from the wonderful: (http://barefootpavee.blogspot.co.uk)

This traditional Traveller caravan was built for Irish music legends The Fureys. It is now owned by 'horsey-man' Johnny Fee (below) who was the creator of my traditional portable hearth and one of the most colourful characters I have met on my own travels.

Market scenes in Derry in the 1900s. Above: Dealers and onlookers gathered at the cattle market/slaughterhouse in the Bogside. Middle: Geese were walked to the city's quayside for shipping to Scotland. Their feet were tarred and sanded for protection on their journey. Bottom: Haymarket sheds near the city docks.

Fair Comments?

I found this interesting snippet in the course of my research into markets and fairs. I pass no comment on its observations of Derry women and how they used to trade. But I agree entirely with the comments about our local butter:

> The women who compose the majority of the market are generally tall and well proportioned; but we look in vain for the plump figure and comely fairness that so eminently distinguish the market-going community in England. Their complexions are tinged by the smoke of their cabins, and their dark keen eyes twinkle upon the purchasers with a shrewd laughing expression, as if they were ever on the alert to take advantage of ignorance or want of judgment . . .
>
> The mutton in appearance approaches to meagreness; yet as an article of food, I have seldom tasted its equal in flavour and quality. The fish-market is admirable; salmon and trout are in the high season; and, in my opinion, they stand first upon the list of northern luxuries . . . There is an abundant supply of fine fresh eggs: turkey's eggs are introduced at the breakfast table, and a great treat they are. Too much cannot be said in commendation of their butter: I have seldom met with this requisite to domestic comfort so sweet, compact, and wholesome, as in Ireland.

(Baldwin and Cradock; and Simkin and Marshall, *Notes of a Journey in the North of Ireland in the Summer of 1827*.)

Markets, 1834

Below is a list of food/produce markets recorded in Derry in 1834. As well as these regular markets there were six annual fairs which were relatively well attended:

- One of the city's oldest recorded markets – a meat market or 'shambles' – was established by Alderman Alexander and held every weekday since 1760 in an area just off Linenhall Street (so named because of the linen market held their every Wednesday from 1770).
- A butter market was established in 1825 and held every weekday in Waterloo Place.
- A fish market established in 1825 and held every weekday in an area just off Linenhall Street.
- A potato market established in 1825 and held in Society Street every weekday.
- A vegetable market (also selling poultry and butter) held just off Linenhall Street every weekday.
- A fruit market held within the Walls between Ferryquay Gate and New Gate every Wednesday and Saturday since 1827.
- A corn market held in Foyle Street every Wednesday and Saturday since 1832.
- A livestock market (cows, pigs, sheep and goats) held near Bishop Street every Wednesday since 1832.
- A slop and pork market held near Linenhall Street every weekday since 1832 selling fresh and salted pork.

Other markets such as yarn, meal, horses, flax and linen were also held throughout the city in various locations.

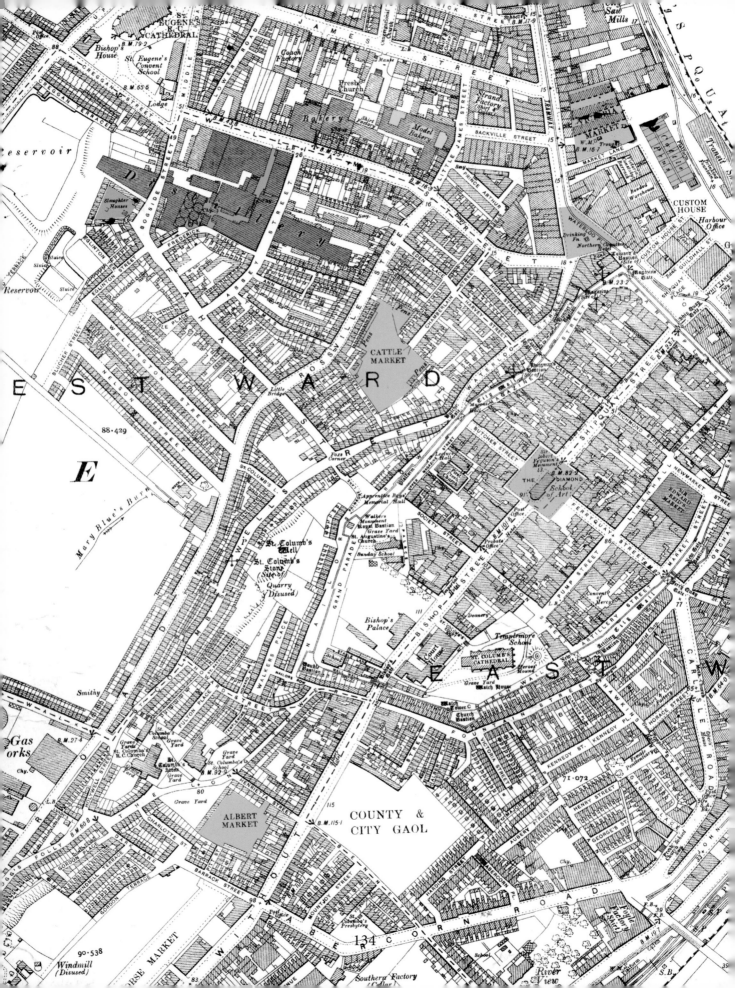

A Developing City

This map, published in 1907, highlights some of the more prominent localities within the city in relation to food/drink produce, manufacturing and retail of the period in question.

Key

- Markets/Fairs
- Pork Stores/Curing House
- Distillery
- Large Bakeries

There are many more shops, warehouses, stores, hotels and restaurants not marked on the map. See Tour Map on page 216-217 for more detail.

137

Flavours of the Foyle

Derry City Council hosts 'Flavours of the Foyle', a major two-day seafood festival, developed in partnership with the Loughs Agency and the wider food tourism industry across the region, including the Irish Food Heritage Project.

Originally established in 2011 – in tandem with the city's Clipper initiative – the Flavours of the Foyle has become a signature event in the city's cultural calendar.

The festival comprises a major boulevard of chefs with 15-20 restaurant-kitchens cooking high-quality seafood, and a chance to try and buy at a major 'theatre of food' with celebrity chefs.

Many of the city and region's finest chefs, restaurants, food producers and seafood suppliers provide culinary advice, samples, demonstrations and much more. The festival also includes street theatre, animation programmes, kids crafts, film, masterchef demos and lectures.

The festival is a chance to celebrate the significant contribution the River Foyle and its associated industries and bounties have made to the wider city in terms of cultural, socio-economic and tourism development and regeneration over the years.

Emmet M'Court
Pan-fried salmon
Boxty crust
Sloke and cockle
sauce

The Walled City Market

The Walled City Market is a speciality food and craft market that takes place on the first Saturday of each month during spring and summer (March to September inclusive). The market takes place in the heart of the city centre in Guildhall Square and within a few yards of the 17th-century historic City Walls and the Guildhall. The market operates from 10.00am to 4.00pm and offers an array of fine goods including cakes, jewellery, art, breads, meats, fruit, vegetables, handmade chocolate and crafts. The market also regularly hosts a variety of food vendors offering a wide range of hot and tasty, speciality and organic foods. The Walled City Market and seasonal continental markets are not to be missed by those who love their street food or traditional handmade confectionery or crafts.

The Great Game Fairs of Ireland

In 2013 the Irish Game Fair & Flavour Fine Food Festival in Northern Ireland combined with its partner in RoI, the Irish Game and Country Fair, and are now marketed as the Great Game Fairs of Ireland.

The team behind the Great Game Fairs of Ireland, along with the good people at Shane's Castle, Birr Castle and Ballywalter Estate, have a fine history and pedigree of delivering successful family-friendly events. In 2013 they combined the Ballywalter Fair and the Shane's Castle event into what is likely to be the largest ever Irish game or country fair.

When the organising team launched the first major Irish Game Fair in 1978 one of their main objectives was promoting the importance of country sports, farming and conservation interests, working together for the preservation of the Irish countryside and the rural way of life.

Over thirty-five years on, that objective is even more relevant, as the traditional rural way of life is increasingly adversely affected by legislation and habitat destruction. The Game Fair team fiercely believe that there is a continuing need for a strong unified voice to promote balance between the various, and sometimes competing, interests of land users within the countryside such as farmers, building industry, country sports, conservation and tourism entities.

The Irish Food Heritage Project and the

Albert and Irene Titterington, founders and organisers of the Great Game Fairs of Ireland.

Great Game Fairs of Ireland share common purpose and work together to help promote and defend what is best in the Irish countryside. With the support of the *Irish Country Sports and Country Life* magazine and help of the www.countrysportsandcountrylife.com online magazine and web portal, it is envisaged that the fairs can play a crucial role in preserving the Irish countryside and its rural traditions while at the same time promoting rural business and tourism.

Whilst always respecting tradition, the organisers of the Great Game Fairs continue to innovate by introducing new attractions and events more enticing to new generations and family audiences. This marketing flair has been

recognised by the Northern Fair being awarded the prestigious Northern Ireland Tourist Board Marketing Excellence Award in 2005.

In addition to the traditional Game Fair attractions, the fairs have a huge range of entertaining and educational activities, displays and attractions to interest anyone who lives, works or plays in the Irish countryside. Apart from the entertainment and educational objectives, the Great Game Fairs of Ireland have hard commercial objectives both for the brand and for their exhibitors ie to create Fairs in Ireland of the size, scope and stature of the best Fairs in the UK and Europe and to deliver the best shop windows for rural products and services in Ireland.

The Irish Food Heritage Project commends the work of the Great Game Fairs of Ireland and continues to attend as many of their events as possible as an exhibitor and a visitor. They truly are a wonderful day out for the family and the perfect way to sample the wares and produce of many of the best local and regional food purveyors that the country has to offer.

CHAPTER 12

The *Titanic* Connection

It's often said that no matter what remote corner of the world you visit you'll run into a native of Derry. The city's reach, it seems, is boundless. But even I was shocked to learn that the chef who created one of the signature dishes for the world famous, and ill-fated, White Star liner RMS *Titanic* had roots in the North West – Albert Sargent.

I first became aware of the story a number of years ago through one of my culinary students at the North West Regional College, Amanda Sargent, a great-niece of the acclaimed chef. Amanda, who subsequently died at a tragically young age, brought in a menu, which had been proudly preserved by her family for 100 years. The menu, from 31 May 1911, celebrates the launch of the *Titanic*, sister ship of the *Olympia*, at Belfast's Grand Central Hotel and features as its main course *Filet de Mouton à la Sargent*. Albert Sargent was the legendary Head Chef of the hotel at the time and this dish was his hallmark. According to Amanda, all the officers of the doomed ship, including the captain, Edward John Smith, and the liner's designer, Thomas Andrews, attended the event, alongside many of the local dignitaries of the day.

Albert Sargent was originally a Cockney but after his spell in Belfast he eventually settled in Derry, where his family still live. His son Albert Junior, who lived in Drumahoe until his death in 2010, went on to become a famous chef in his own right. He trained at

Amanda Sargent, a great-niece of legendary Head Chef Albert Sargent.

the Melville and City hotels in Derry before working in a number of the Great Railway hotels across Ireland.

I met with Downpatrick-born chef Graham McClements, who as a 14-year-old trainee worked under Albert Junior at the Slieve Donard Hotel in 1969, and he remembered him very fondly: 'Albert had a well-known, now famous, father who was a renowned chef and had a lot to do with putting together the menu for the *Titanic*'s maiden voyage. Although I'm not sure that Albert really boasted about this, I always felt that there might have been a bit of aggro between them. Of course, it might just have been the normal father and teenage son thing. I do remember that Albert did have a few signature dishes and I'm sure one of these was the mutton dish. He was a

RMS *Titanic*.

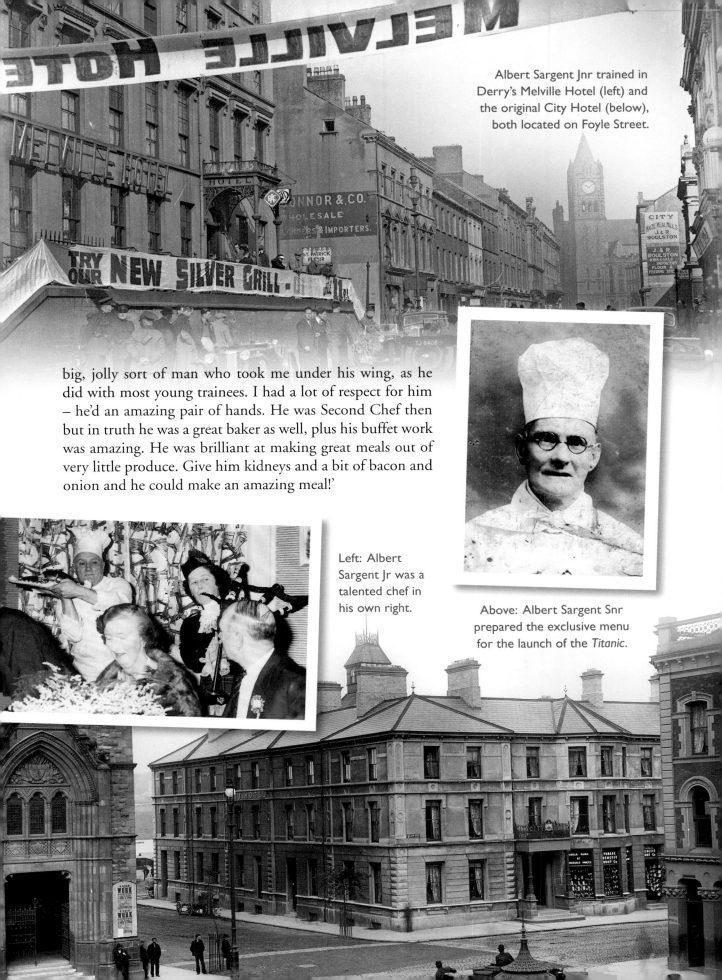

Albert Sargent Jnr trained in Derry's Melville Hotel (left) and the original City Hotel (below), both located on Foyle Street.

big, jolly sort of man who took me under his wing, as he did with most young trainees. I had a lot of respect for him – he'd an amazing pair of hands. He was Second Chef then but in truth he was a great baker as well, plus his buffet work was amazing. He was brilliant at making great meals out of very little produce. Give him kidneys and a bit of bacon and onion and he could make an amazing meal!'

Left: Albert Sargent Jr was a talented chef in his own right.

Above: Albert Sargent Snr prepared the exclusive menu for the launch of the *Titanic*.

Above: RMS *Titanic* under construction in the Harland & Wolff shipyard in Belfast.
Below: An illustration of a dining room in the *Titanic*.

Expensive Menus!

A menu for the *Titanic* launch in Belfast, featuring Albert (Senior) Sargent's dish, sold at auction for £36,000 in November 2012. The document had been saved for posterity by one of the 69 guests attending the champagne event.

A second menu from the day the *Titanic* began its maiden voyage, 10 April 1912, was sold at the same auction for £64,000. It had been taken by two first-class passengers, fishmongers Richard and Stanley May, who luckily got off the ship at Queenstown (Cobh), before it set off on its doomed Atlantic journey.

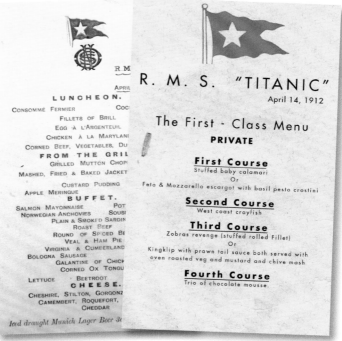

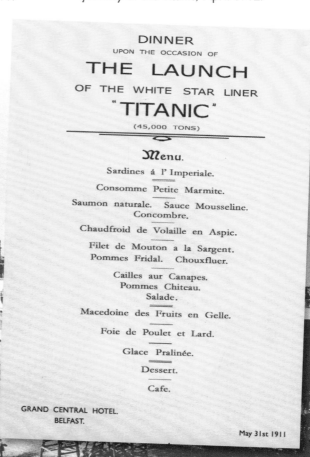

Below: The menu from the launch party of the *Titanic* in the Grand Central Hotel in Belfast on 31 May 1911.

Above: The menu from the maiden journey of the *Titanic*, April 1912.

LUNCHEON

UPON THE OCCASION OF

THE LAUNCH

OF

THE WHITE STAR LINER

"TITANIC"

(45.000 TONS).

SISTER SHIP TO THE "OLYMPIC."

THE LARGEST STEAMERS IN THE WORLD.

MAY 31ST. 1911.

GRAND CENTRAL HOTEL.
BELFAST.

DINNER

UPON THE OCCASION OF

THE LAUNCH

OF THE WHITE STAR LINER

"TITANIC"

(45,000 TONS)

Menu.

Sardines á l' Imperiale.

Consomme Petite Marmite.

Saumon naturale. Sauce Mousseline.
Concombre.

Chaudfroid de Volaille en Aspic.

Filet de Mouton a la Sargent.
Pommes Fridal. Chouxfluer.

Cailles aur Canapes.
Pommes Chiteau.
Salade.

Macedoine des Fruits en Gelle.

Foie de Poulet et Lard.

Glace Pralinée.

Dessert.

Cafe.

GRAND CENTRAL HOTEL.
BELFAST.

May 31st 1911

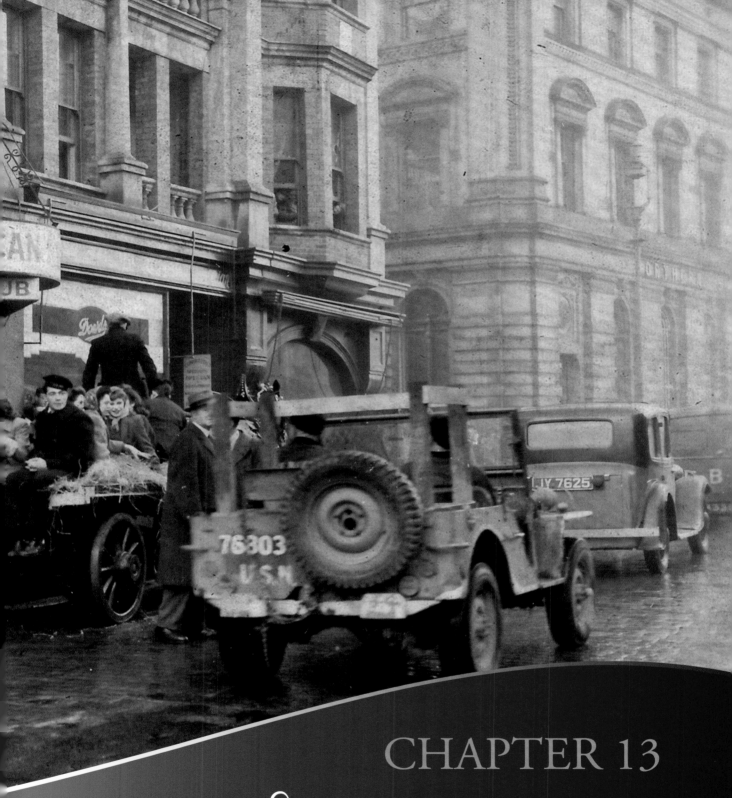

CHAPTER 13

War Years, Immigration and Smuggling (1900s)

Luigi Macari, pictured with a customer at his Central Café in William Street in the 1950s.

The early part of the 20ᵗʰ century saw the North West's food tastes develop a cosmopolitan flavour as immigrants arrived from across Europe and beyond, bringing their unique culinary skills with them. Prominent among them were a number of families from southern Italy – including the Fiorentini, the Macari, the Yannarelli, the Morelli and the Battisti families – who would go on to run ice-cream shops and cafés right up to the present day. Morelli's has been in business in Coleraine and Portstewart since 1911, while Fiorentini's has been operating in Derry since 1912.

The first to arrive in Derry, according to the *Derry Journal*, were the Macari family in 1897. Luigi Macari began his business 'tramp-ing the streets', selling ice cream from a hand-cart. His granddaughter, Libra Marchant, said it wasn't long before he had enough money to buy a shop in William Street, which was run by his two sons.

According to the *Journal* of 21 April 2011: 'In the early days, ice-cream making was a laborious business with much of the mixing having to be done by hand. In fact, to ensure there would be enough ice cream for the day ahead – particularly during the summer – work could begin as early as 5.00 AM. A key element of the ice-cream making process was coating the mixing bowl with large pieces of rock salt – the only known way of preventing the ice cream from melting. Indeed, Libra Marchant vividly recalls once putting the rock salt into the ice

Left: Macari's was one of the city's first Italian ice-cream salons in the 1950s.
Above & below: Fiorentini's Café carries on the Italian ice-cream tradition in the city to this day.

cream instead of into the bowl – in the process ruining an entire day's supply.'

Despite their expertise, there were some foodstuffs the Italian community could not prepare in their new home, so they would send orders to London regularly for treats such as salami and special cheeses.

In 1940, as a result of Mussolini declaring war on Britain and France, some Italians from the North West were deported as 'aliens', while others such as Jimmy Macari from Derry were interned on the Isle of Man. The Macari family business survived until the start of the 1970s, which saw William Street badly hit by the Troubles.

Fiorentini's Café is still run by the family and is now situated on Strand Road. It was hard work getting established and surviving over the decades but it bore dividends. Michael Fiorentini remembers his grandfather riding his bike to Buncrana, thirteen miles away, and selling 4,000 wafers of ice cream a day in the summer.

Saffron: the Nagra family Indian restaurant and café on Clarendon Street.

There were times, however, that even the greatest entrepreneurs were stumped. During the Troubles, the frontage of Fiorentini's landmark building was completely destroyed in an explosion on Strand Road. As the family began the clean-up, a customer stepped through the window and asked them: 'Are you open?'

A small contingent of Jews who had been expelled from Russia settled in Derry at the start of the 20th century. A synagogue was established at Kennedy Place in the Fountain and kosher food was prepared under the guidance of a rabbi. The community had largely died out by the 1940s, though a second wave arrived from Austria during World War II.

The late 1940s saw the first influx of Indians to Derry, following the British withdrawal from India and the creation of Pakistan. The new arrivals sought employment primarily in the retail sector, but a number of them opened food outlets and several are still in operation today. Initially, they found it difficult to source spices in the North West and were forced to travel to Belfast, and even London, to acquire their ingredients. They also found the local produce a little difficult to adapt to. Ravinda Sumra recalls his father telling him that Derry women had to give them lessons in cooking potatoes when they first arrived.

Suki Nagra's family moved to Derry from India in 1965. His mother worked in the shirt factories for many years, while his father sold clothes door-to-door and eventually opened a shop in Carlisle Road. Suki had a keen interest in cooking from an early age and while studying in Manchester University, near the curry

mile of Rusholme, he was inspired to introduce Indian food to the general public of his home town, establishing the India House restaurant in Carlisle Road in 1984. Suki eventually closed these premises and opened a new restaurant in Clarendon Street – Saffron – in late 2013.

Currently, more than 200 people of Indian origin live in Derry, which now has its own Sikh temple at Clooney Terrace.

The first Chinese people began arriving in the North West in the 1960s, following the Commonwealth Immigrants Act of 1962, and the majority of them began working in the catering industry. Currently, it's estimated that there are well over 500 Chinese restaurants in Northern Ireland.

The new settlers helped broaden the traditional North West palate, no doubt, but there were other factors as well. Higher wages and cheaper flights allowed more people to enjoy foreign holidays, and this in turn meant our tastes were becoming more adventurous. It also led to the expectation of a higher standard of food at home and better service.

Importantly, too, the idea of eating out meaning a 'good feed' with plentiful portions, was changing as diners sought a more social and luxurious experience. Also, Irish chefs began travelling further afield, nationally and internationally, to get experience – including Letterkenny's Conrad Gallagher, celebrity chef Paul Rankin, and Noel McMeel, formerly of the Beech Hill, and yours truly. Many of these culinary travellers then opened up their own restaurants offering multi-ethnic dishes when they returned to the region.

World War II Boomtown

Derry's location as the furthest Allied port in Europe from Germany (and hence hardest to bomb) and the closest Allied port to the US and Canada, led to the city becoming possibly the most important naval centre of World War II.

In terms of our food heritage, it proved to be a hugely exciting time, with an influx of new dishes courtesy of visiting navies – none more so than the Americans, who made the city their first European base and centre of all radio operations. The GIs loved the city, comparing it to their favourite US vacation spot, Coney Island. And before long, they were converting the locals to the joys of sloppy joes, pizzas, hamburgers, hot dogs, Hershey chocolate, chewing gum and coffee.

The war had prompted food rationing across the North, but the porous border with the Free State, as it was then known, meant that there was wholesale smuggling. And for many years there was a thriving black market in commodities like tea, butter, meat, sugar, eggs and whiskey.

American navy personnel and general infantry men frequented many of Derry's bars, tearooms and cafés and the ever-popular American Red Cross Service Club in Waterloo Place.

Virtually everything was smuggled, from bars of soap to bicycles and cars. Margaret Gilpin, who grew up in Lifford in the 1940s, recalled: 'The women used to smuggle the butter by flattening it and putting it up their jumpers. Flour was concealed in pillowcases tied around the waist and tobacco was put into bags containing two pounds of sugar, which was allowed across the [border] bridge.'

Live animals were sometimes smuggled across the border into the South. One particularly inventive lady dressed a goose she had just purchased in Derry market in baby clothes and hid it in a pram, tying the goose's beak to stop it from squawking. She then took it on the Lough Swilly train and succeeded in transporting it across the frontier to Buncrana.

US navy personnel lining the streets in honour of a royal visit to the city in the 1950s.

CHRISTMAS MENU

December 25, 1943

UNITED STATES NAVAL OPERATING BASE
LONDONDERRY, NORTHERN IRELAND

MENU

TURKEY NOODLE SOUP   CRACKERS

ROAST YOUNG TURKEY

BREAD DRESSING   CRANBERRY SAUCE

GIBLET GRAVY

MASHED POTATOES   CREAMED PEAS

BUTTERED ASPARAGUS

CANDIED YAMS   RIPE OLIVES

MINCED CABBAGE SALAD

MAYONNAISE

HOT ROLLS   COFFEE

PUMPKIN PIE   FRUIT CAKE

CIGARS   CIGARETTES

Above: A 1943 Christmas menu from the US naval operations base in Derry shows the variety of foods available to the naval personnel in service in the city. Many of these foods would be new to locals and very difficult to source during wartime.

Below: The US navy had a presence in the city for many years after the war. Here, servicemen and their families attend a barbecue with free hotdogs and burgers for all.

Childhood Memories of the War Years (1939—1945)

One of Derry's best-loved storytellers Phil Cunningham recounts his memories of growing up in wartime Derry and beyond, and recalls the food and shops of the time and the resourcefulness of a hard-pressed community.

All basic household commodities were scarce during the war years and every family had an official government ration book. A ration coupon was handed to the shopkeeper along with some money to purchase items such as tea, sugar, tobacco, snuff and clothing, when they were available.

The Irish Republic was neutral during the war and Derry people travelled to and fro across the border that was only three miles from the city to smuggle household essentials by bus, bicycle and train. Many people walked the few miles to County Donegal, usually in the late evening when darkness was falling where the British Customs and Excise Authorities set up checkpoints to catch people taking their meagre purchases home and often confiscated any goods they discovered. It was a form of highway robbery because there were many stories about confiscated goods being taken home by some of the customs men for their own use.

People took the train to get some goods for themselves and their neighbours. When they were returning they sometimes hung their shopping bags full of contraband on the outside door handles of the train, on the side away from the station platform, so the customs men wouldn't find them when they came aboard to search. Sometimes a suspicious official looked out of the window and spotted the full shopping bags, and sometimes he pretended not to see them and waved to the train driver to continue on his journey to sighs of relief from the nervous passengers.

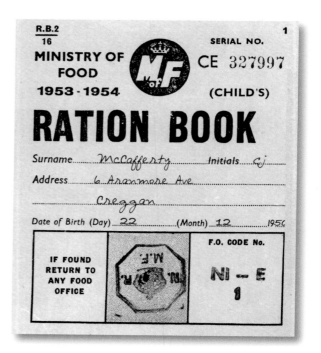

A child's post-war ration book from Derry in the early 1950s.

Every Saturday, the buttermilk carts came into Derry from Donegal. When the horse-drawn cart came into our street, the women queued up to fill their tin cans and jugs with buttermilk and to buy a pound or two of homemade country butter. The buttermilk tasted delicious and my mother or aunt used it when making scone bread.

I learned in later years that those drivers and horses were on the roads to Derry from two and three o'clock in the morning in order to sell their buttermilk, eggs and butter. As butter was rationed during the war, the only person in our household lucky enough to have it on his bread at times was my father whenever it was available.

Margarine was eaten most of the time and whenever it was scarce, people melted suet, which was a solid piece of animal fat. When the suet cooled down, it was poured into a jam jar and then used for spreading like butter on the bread or to fry with in the pan.

The bread vans were horse drawn, as were the coal carts, and in the early mornings the clip clop of the milkman's horse and the

An Old City Dairy horse-drawn float from the 1940s.

clinking of the milk bottles echoed off Derry's Walls as his cart came into the street. Our milkman was Jim Gillespie who also owned a bar on Duke Street in the Waterside. Hugh Gillen from Union Street, and his son Willie, delivered our coal.

The Henry family, who lived up the street in one of the six smaller houses in Nailor's Row, owned a pony and trap and went to all the fairs that were held in the outlying towns. They were also the only family in the area to own a motorcar. It was a big black one with high round mudguards and headlights sticking up at the front. The windows were tinted a dark amber and it had side running boards to stand on to get in or out. It was used as a taxi, and one day we went to Rathmullan in it, a long journey of thirty or forty miles in those times, to visit our mother's cousins.

Old Mrs Henry sold toffee apples and paper pokes of toffee popcorn for a penny, and sometimes we would find a dead cockroach stuck in the toffee. Of course we just poked it out and ate our popcorn. Nowadays, people would probably try to sue for mental distress or something if they found a dead bug in their food but nobody bothered much then.

The Old City Dairy

The Old City Dairy on the Letterkenny Road was for many years a successful family-run business which supplied much of the populace of the Bogside area and beyond with freshly bottled milk.

The old horse-drawn milk floats were a common sight around the city and further afield with their friendly staff delivering their wares in the early morning, rain or shine.

The industry changed in the 1950s and '60s when milk lorries were employed on the main routes. Competition from other providers and the availability through supermarkets led to an eventual decline in the business.

In 1974 the Old City Dairy Ltd on Foyle Road was acquired by Leckpatrick and operated successfully until it wound up in the early 1990s.

American servicemen purchasing milk from roundsman Joe Lynch operating Robert McCarter's float outside Boomhall House in the Culmore Road area of Derry in 1944.

During those war years, 1939 to 1945, fruit was also a scarce commodity in the shops and in October, lorries came from Armagh loaded with apples from the orchards. Whenever one came into our street everybody queued to buy a bucketful for a shilling. It was a great treat to eat a couple of juicy apples or to get a piece of apple pie that my mother baked in the fire oven. Sometimes she would give us a piece of dough that was left over and we would make a couple of small apple tarts to cook along with the cakes or pies.

After the war had ended, a variety of fruits started to arrive in the shops. On one occasion my older brother Paddy, who drove a fruit lorry for Bannigan's stores on Foyle Street, brought home a bunch of bananas. He gave me one and I began to eat it without removing the skin; it tasted horrible! After he stopped laughing and told me that it had to be peeled I enjoyed the taste of it. The only place I had seen bananas before was in the school geography books about Africa.

Bigger's Pork Stores on Foyle Street slaughtered pigs and cured the meat. We were sent there once a week to buy chain bones, pig's feet, ribs and sometimes a pig's cheek or a piece of liver. The meat was greasy but tasty when cooked along with potatoes and cabbage.

There were no fridges so the groceries were bought daily. We got most of our provisions from McHugh's shop on Bishop Street and sometimes from Pat Hegarty's on Walker's Square. John McHugh's grocery shop had a barrel of salted fish outside the front door, and inside had hams and dried ling fish hanging from the ceiling. Everything was sold loose and scooped out of the storage bins to be weighed and poured into brown paper bags; items such as sugar, tea, flour, and barley, peas and lentils for making soup.

All of the grocery stores were the same and the mixed smells of everything together in the shop were overpowering at times. None of these shops sold milk which had to be bought from Arthur Breslin's dairy shop in Bishop Street, where one could also buy cheeses and other dairy products.

In the warm weather, when we bought butter and margarine, we stored them in a box with a wire netting door. The wire kept the cats and rats and birds from eating the contents. The box was hung on the wall in the shadiest and coolest place in the back yard as it was the only way the butter could be kept from melting.

In the mornings, we went down to Sonny Fleming's Bakery on Rossville Street to get a

dozen baps. Sonny made the tastiest baps in Derry and people came from all over the town to queue up to buy them. I didn't like the ones with the caraway seed in them that were known locally as 'carvy baps'.

Further down Bishop Street from McHugh's was John Gibbon's butcher shop where my mother bought the mince for some of our daily dinners and the sausages for my father's Sunday breakfast. Beside Gibbon's was Mrs Murray's small confectionery shop that never seemed to have many sweets displayed in the window or on the shelves. Next door was Hunter's Rock Bakery Company bread shop where we purchased some of our bread. James McGirr sold fruit and vegetables beside Hunter's Bakery where we were able to get a limited amount of greens and potatoes

The Hippsley family ran a small general shop and grocers in Bishop Street in the 1960s and 1970s.

daily. Above the shop door and windows was a sun canopy to protect and keep the vegetables that were displayed outside cool and fresh. The shop was owned in later years by Elizabeth and William Hippsley.

Long-gone pubs, grocers and butchers shops from old Derry.

People often found it cheaper to buy goods across the border than in the local Derry shops, like those above, during the post-war years and subsequently casual smuggling became a way of life.

The Black Huts, Smuggling and Water Rats

On Sunday evenings quite a few men, women and boys walked the three miles across the border into County Donegal to buy cigarettes and other commodities that were cheaper to buy there than in Derry in the early 1950s. The authorities frowned on the activities and called it smuggling.

Due to lack of housing, some people living here and there along the border who owned small pieces of ground built small two-roomed wooden huts, roofed with tarred black felt, to live in with their young families. Willie White opened a shop which was the original 'Black Hut', just across the border near Killea, and it became the favourite spot for buying butter, sugar and fresh eggs. A big tasty bar of Cowan's cream toffee with twelve squares in it was the most popular treat nearly everybody brought over if there was enough money left after buying all of the more essential items. We would eat a few squares on the way home and then try to keep some for whenever we went to the pictures on Monday night.

In 1952 Johnny Doherty opened a shop. He lived just over the border at the Killea reservoir, and it, too, became known as the Black Hut.

The NI customs men patrolling the border roads in cars were called the 'Water Rats' and they frequently set up surprise checkpoints to catch petty smugglers, especially on Sunday evenings. People were searched for goods and many of them had their meagre quantities of cigarettes or tobacco confiscated. Women with prams were sometimes asked to remove their babies so the prams could be searched, and any items that shouldn't have been in there were taken by the Water Rats. Everyone regarded them as highway robbers.

The legal amounts the Northern customs allowed to be taken across the border were twenty cigarettes, a pound of butter, two ounces of snuff or tobacco and some tea and sugar. After a while, everyone learned to watch out for the customs men and warned each other when they were about.

My friends and I used to purchase commodities in the Black Hut for the people in our street and we went there a couple of evenings a week when it was dark. It was easier then to see the headlights of the customs men's car whenever we were walking back along the dark road from the Black Hut with our messages. A couple of times we were caught and the goods taken from us whenever the Water Rats got crafty. They parked with no lights on at the side of the road and whenever they heard us coming along, chatting and unaware of their presence, they switched on the full beams and blinded us. It wasn't a very pleasant feeling whenever we had to tell our neighbours that the meagre goods they had spent their last few shillings on were taken by the Water Rats.

An old yarn tells us about the man who crossed over the border to the six counties on a bicycle twice every day and was stopped each time and searched by the Water Rats, but he never was found to be carrying any contraband. A few years later, whenever the prices got more favourable to buy goods in the North of Ireland, he met a customs man in Derry who asked why he cycled over the border twice a day and never smuggled anything. The man cheerfully replied that he got the bus down and was smuggling the bicycles back up.

(Extracts from *Derry Down the Days*, by Phil Cunningham, published by Guildhall Press, 2002, and *Echoes of Derry* by Phil Cunningham, published by Guildhall Press, 2003.)

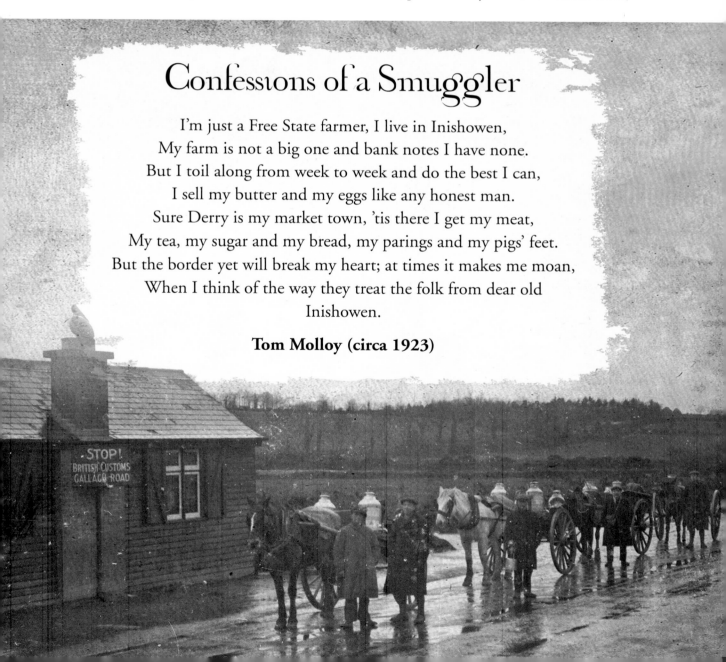

Confessions of a Smuggler

I'm just a Free State farmer, I live in Inishowen,
My farm is not a big one and bank notes I have none.
But I toil along from week to week and do the best I can,
I sell my butter and my eggs like any honest man.
Sure Derry is my market town, 'tis there I get my meat,
My tea, my sugar and my bread, my parings and my pigs' feet.
But the border yet will break my heart; at times it makes me moan,
When I think of the way they treat the folk from dear old
Inishowen.

Tom Molloy (circa 1923)

The Perils of Smuggling

For almost a century, food smuggling was a daily occurrence along the Derry-Donegal border which marks the frontier between the North and the South of Ireland. And for many years, all types of equipment used in the preparation and storage of food were much cheaper in the North. Maud Rainey, a colleague at the North West Regional College, set up home in the South – but ran into difficulties when she tried to bring a fridge across the border. This is Maud's story:

It was October 1983. We had just got married in July and we were slowly but surely building our home together. Times were tough, we had a big mortgage and we were saving for each new item, which hadn't been given as wedding presents. The old fridge that a generous friend had bequeathed to us had just broken down so we investigated the purchase of a new one. Since we were living in Buncrana, the obvious place to buy was Derry for choice and price. But remembering we would have to declare the sale on crossing the border, the bargain from Derry didn't seem as appealing, as a tax levy would be slapped on.

My friend was married to a tax officer so we hatched a plan. She would find out from her husband when the customs post would close and if there were any mobile patrols on specific nights. It was established that the best route would be through Killea on a Thursday night after 10.00pm. We had never been on this road before but got clear directions from friends and family. The fridge was purchased and a good deal was got. My brother lent us a trailer and the clandestine operation began.

We set fourth, two very nervous smugglers with our brand new fridge towards Killea. About two miles outside the city, on a still dark night, we were suddenly flagged down by two British Army patrols. Lights flashing, soldiers with blackened faces; I swore I'd never, ever do anything like this again for the value of £50 at that. It transpired we had a tail light missing in the trailer and the number plate could not be seen. We looked suspicious but when we explained, the soldier just laughed at the thought of our innocent pursuit.

So onwards and over the border we travelled, past the tiny unmanned customs post and we both breathed a sigh of relief. 'Ah – maybe we *would* try this again, it was easy!' But to our horror, the road ahead was blocked. There was a car parked across the road and customs officers appeared out of hedges shining flashlights! We slowed down and rolled down the window.

'Excuse me, Madame . . .'

And it was then that I recognised the voice – my friend's husband and his colleagues had decided to set up an impromptu checkpoint to scare the life out of us! Needless to say I vowed never to try a stunt like that again!

The Golden Teapot

Faller's Jewellers on Strand Road is the new home for the city's iconic Golden Teapot, which was originally created in 1866 to advertise John Parkhill's new grocery business in Waterloo Place. The teapot hung above the store for almost 100 years – even surviving two bullet holes in the 1920s. McCullagh Grocers then took over the store, where the teapot hung until 1969. Today, it is a proud reminder of Derry's historic reputation for hospitality.

The teapot is made from copper with 24-carat gold leaf. Steam spouts from the teapot on the hour every hour in daylight. The Golden Teapot rivals one across the Atlantic, which commemorates the Boston Tea Party during the American War of Independence. The Boston Tea Kettle and the Golden Teapot are identical in size.

A City with a Farming Pedigree

Although it has now almost completely faded from our civic memory, the city of Derry was, until the 1970s, the hub of the agricultural industry in the North West of Ireland, gathering-in, processing and exporting huge amounts of beef, pork, mutton, hides and dairy products. Until then, urban Derry had largely kept itself within the city limits, as defined in Victorian times. The flat and gently sloping land immediately around the city contained numerous farms, large and small, which served the daily needs of the city, supplying the fresh food and produce to help feed its citizens and the many workers of the thriving shirt and engineering industries.

Kilfennan Farm is but one example of a farm within the liberties of Derry. Located on a deep loamy soil, less that two miles from the city, the farm was well-suited to producing the rich grass needed for quality milk production. In the late 1700s the farm had been owned by the Mackys. When they emigrated to New Zealand in the 1840s, the farm was sold to the Glenns, famous at the Derry Show for their prizewinning pigs. Eventually in 1923 the farm was bought by Herbert and Annie Lusby. Annie came from Irish farming stock near Desertmartin in the south of the county; Herbert was the second son of a dairy farmer from near Beverley in the East Riding of Yorkshire. They started with four crossbred dairy shorthorn cows. They also had two horses which not only tilled the fields but also pulled a cart each day to the city to make the deliveries of milk to Herbert and Annie's first customers. Annie raised hens and often the money from the eggs was the primary source of income to invest in new stock and machinery. By the 1970s, the dairy herd had increased to 120 pedigree Ayrshire and Friesian milking cows. Delivery of fresh milk directly from farm to customers had ended with the formation of the Milk Marketing Board in 1955, and milk from the farm was delivered in milk churns, and then latterly bulk tankers, from Kilfennan Farm to the Leckpatrick Dairy at Rossdowney.

The demand for new housing in the 1970s has swallowed up most of the fertile land within the city liberties, which once served the immediate needs of the Derry workers for fresh produce. On Sundays the congregation of Kilfennan Presbyterian Church now worship where Lusbys' cows once grazed on gentle slopes. Supermarket vans now speed along the Rossdowney Road making deliveries to the homes of internet shoppers where once the Dupont workers, taking a short-cut along the same country road, would have to wait until the twice-daily traffic jam, created by Lusbys' cows moving between milking parlour and field, had cleared.

Our foods are now transported over longer distances. But there is a move in the present-day hinterland of the city of Derry to develop food products which are local and which reconnect the people of this great city with the farms which produce the food they eat.

Latest type sterilizing plant installed to ensure bottles & utensils clean & germ free

BOUGHT OF

AYRSHIRE DAIRY

LICENSED   PRODUCERS OF   GRADE B MILK

HERBERT LUSBY
KILFENNAN, WATERSIDE, LONDONDERRY

Below: 'Oft did the harvest to her sickle yield.' Miss Jane Clark of Raphoe, aged 95, who, for many years unaided, cut and gathered in her corn crop.

John Brewster, Bread and Biscuit Manufacturer

The following was published in the late nineteenth century in the *Londonderry Sentinel* and describes the state-of-the-art processes employed by Brewster's Bakery at the time, when the business was at its peak:

Mr Brewster's 'Model Bakery' is one of the recognised institutions of domestic industry in Derry. It is now nearly six years since this enterprising gentleman created a sensation (and a pleasurable sensation, too) in Derry by opening his Model Bakery, although the business was first established in Londonderry in the year 1872 upon a scale of completeness in equipment which was not surpassed anywhere at the time.

All the latest improvements in the shape of machinery and appliances for the clean and scientific making and baking of bread were brought into requisition in this well-named Model Bakery, which we may here

mention is entirely lit by the electric light; and since the place first came into active operation it has been further improved from time to time in several of its most important features. Early in 1889 Mr Brewster made another move in advance, and immensely increased the volume of this business and the public usefulness of his establishment by the addition of a large and splendidly appointed biscuit manufactory. This very important annexe to the other premises in James Street has made the entire place one of the largest and most interesting establishments of its kind in the kingdom. We should be carried far beyond the limits of space imposed upon us here did we attempt to describe in detail the various fittings and special features of this new biscuit bakery, but we need hardly say that, like the bread bakery, it is absolutely up to date in every respect.

Indeed, there are many special arrangements here which we have not seen in any other bakery, and all the machinery and appliances bear the names of makers whose reputation is widely recognised and whose work is unimpeachable. So far as we can judge, there is not a fault to be found with Mr Brewster's establishment as it now stands. The conditions under which the baking industry is here carried on are of a character satisfying every requirement in cleanliness and hygiene, and at the same time they are favourable to the attainment of the very best results in the goods produced.

Mr Brewster's resources enable him to turn out with equal ease great quantities of the finest biscuit confectionery and immense supplies of plain and fancy bread of every kind. His bakeries are equally well adapted for the production of the most delicate wafer biscuits, the substantial ship's biscuit, and the homely household loaf. The 'gay Sally Lunn' and 'the rollicking bun' (as Mr Gilbert has it) are duly represented in the output of this house, in company with countless other toothsome members of the great family of bakers' wares; and in all cases the public find to their satisfaction that the high standard of purity and quality with which the name of Brewster is worthily associated in this trade is fully and adequately maintained.

We need hardly add the self-evident information that Mr John Brewster does an immense and steadily increasing business, giving employment to a very large force of hands. The success of his undertaking was a foregone conclusion almost from the day of its inception, and none of the confidence so honestly gained is likely to be forfeited as long as Mr Brewster retains the helm of the concern in his own capable hands. Those who are at all interested in the progress of the trade in Derry will not be slow to agree with us, and with many others who have visited the Model Bakery in James Street, that this establishment in all its aspects is no less a credit to the charming city on the Foyle than it is to the enterprising citizen who has so vigorously and successfully organised and developed it. Telegrams for the house we have herein briefly reviewed should be addressed 'Brewster, Derry' and the telephone number of the Model Bakery is 37.

"OFTEN BUTTERED NEVER BETTERED"

Brewster's Bakery horse-drawn carts on display at the city showgrounds.

EAT BREWSTERS' BREAD

MADE BY

THE MOST UP-TO-DATE

MACHINERY

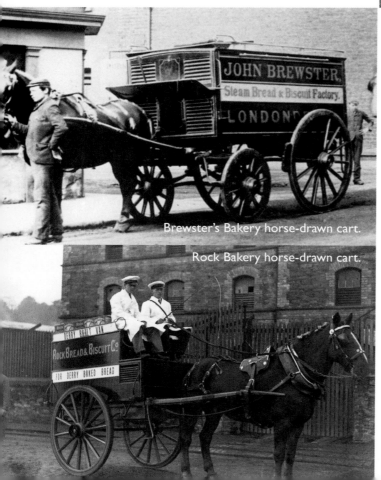

Brewster's Bakery horse-drawn cart.

Rock Bakery horse-drawn cart.

WATERSIDE BAKERY.

BREAD of Superior Quality.

MACHINERY of the best description introduced.

Sole Agent in Londonderry for

"OLIVER'S Patent BROWN BREAD."

ROBERT OLIVER, MORPETH, PATENTEE.

OLIVER EATON

4, Duke Street, Derry.

Above: Eaton & Co
Waterside Bakery, Duke
Street, Derry, c.1900.
Below: Stevenson's Bakery,
William Street, Derry.

STEVENSONS LTD.

Famous for their

Bread • Pure Confectionery

Unequalled Restaurant Service

●

Restaurants

STEVENSONS
Waterloo Place

THOMPSONS
Ferryquay Street

LONDONDERRY

The Old City Docks

This account, taken from the Londonderry Port and Harbour Commission's excellent website www.londonderryport.com, details the significant changes affecting the city as a port over the generations.

The emigration trade established Derry as one of the chief Irish ports for transatlantic trade in the 18th century. In 1771 the American colonies took more linen cloth and provisions from Derry than Britain did, and 30% of Ulster-Scots emigrants, about 75,000 people, departed though Derry port to North America prior to 1776.

By the early 19th century, Derry had become one of the most important and thriving ports in Ireland. In 1835, the value of exports from Derry exceeded £1 million, making her the fifth largest port in Ireland. By the 1820s, considerable quantities of beef, butter, pork, ham, bacon, oatmeal and flax were exported to Britain through Derry.

Emigration from Ireland fell dramatically from 1931 as legislation ending uncontrolled immigration to the US became fully operational. The outbreak of war in 1939 meant the end of this emigrant trade. With the return of peace, the transatlantic liners did not come back to Derry. Train loads of emigrants from all over Ireland instead headed for Cobh.

Derry's cross-channel trade was the port's core business and it displayed steady, if not dramatic, growth during the 19th century and into the early 20th century. In this period,

inward coastal tonnages rose from around 200,000 tons in 1860 to just under 300,000 tons by 1910. Cross-channel traffic remained high in the inter-war years.

The cross-channel passenger trade from Derry was at its peak in 1910. At this time, a passenger steamer left Derry for England six times a week.

The decline in passenger services to England began in 1912 when the service to Fleetwood ended. Ten years later, in 1922, the steamers to Liverpool ceased carrying passengers but continued as cargo and livestock

boats until 27 September 1965. The Heysham steamers stopped carrying passengers in the early 1930s but remained in operation for cargo until 11 October 1963.

The export of livestock was crucial to the growth and prosperity of cross-channel trade. In 1884, 57,623 cattle, 14,791 sheep and 19,305 pigs were exported through Derry to English and Scottish ports. Livestock exports continued to prosper through the interwar years. Cattle exports, for example, to the ports of Glasgow, Heysham and Liverpool, through Derry, jumped from 49,280 in 1918 to 91,000 in 1924.

The backbone of foreign trade in the interwar years continued to be large shipments of maize from north and south America, initially destined for Watts Distillery but increasingly as a cheap source of animal feed, and William McCorkell & Co. became one of its chief suppliers. The other major foreign import was timber, now coming as often from Norway and Sweden as from Canada.

From the 1960s it was becoming clear that the city-centre location of the port was not sustainable for long-term development. Ship sizes had changed so much that the quays were no longer suitable for larger vessels.

In the 1960s, William McCorkell, the main grain importer for animal feed, received its grain from America via Liverpool. The grain came to Liverpool in large ships from America and was then transferred to smaller ships, carrying some 6,000 tons of grain, which could berth at McCorkell's Mill at Queen's Quay.

In 1976 the decision was made to permanently close the dry dock (which had opened in 1862) at Rock Quay as the demand for this facility was very slight. This area, known as Meadowbank, was now developed by the Harbour Commissioners. From the early 1980s until the move to Lisahally, Derry port was based at Meadowbank.

By 1990 it was clear that the future prosperity of Derry port was dependent upon relocation four miles downstream to a deep-water facility at Lisahally in order to provide capacity for larger vessels and opportunities to acquire more land for expansion.

The deep-water port now has the capacity to handle large vessels of over 30,000 tonnes and manage bulk cargoes. Furthermore, owing to its geographic location, and with facilities in place for future expansion, the port has the ability to serve the entire western seaboard of Ireland.

CRAIGALLIAN
GLASGOW

Scenes from the life
and times of the old
Derry docks.

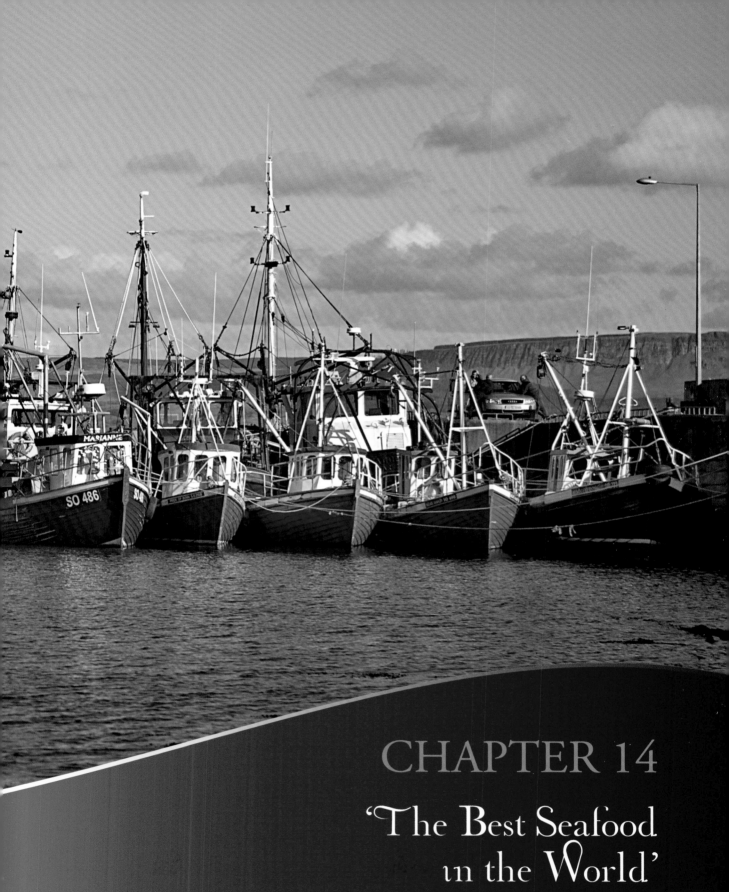

CHAPTER 14

'The Best Seafood
in the World'

Kealy's Seafood Restaurant in Greencastle, County Donegal.

Greencastle in County Donegal has been the hub of the North West seafood tradition for centuries, but the port's international reputation has skyrocketed over the past couple of decades with the opening of Kealy's Bar & Restaurant in 1989. Its clients range from poets to playwrights to presidents. And this author also was lucky to be able to spend some very happy times there over the years.

I left the Catering College in Portrush, County Antrim, in 1991, having divided my energies between my studies there and completing my three-year apprenticeship as commis chef at the Everglades Hotel in Prehen. At the time, I was hearing news of a terrific new restaurant that was leading the way in nouvelle cuisine. Gastronomes, critics and food lovers from all over the country were travelling to this small seafood bar in Greencastle to sample its *fruits de mer*. And all of this was on my own doorstep in Inishowen. I just had to work there!

The business was set up by husband-and-wife team James (now sadly deceased) and Patricia Kealy. They had met at Killybegs Catering College, before taking over the Kealy family pub from James's parents – a pub which they would transform into Ireland's top seafood establishment.

I had the privilege of joining Kealy's in the summer of 1991, as commis chef, at the height of the restaurant's success. Back then it was a small establishment, dimly lit and with a seating capacity of about 44, although there was a back room which could accommodate up to another 12 people or so. It featured a homely, roaring fire and traditional music. And when full to capacity, it would give you the impression that the whole of the tiny village of Greencastle was celebrating.

At Kealy's I had the opportunity to cook many wonderful and unusual fish and shellfish, like the ferocious-looking sea wolf, which has a head and large teeth like an American pit-bull terrier, but which boasts the most beautiful flavoured and tender flesh. I was also introduced to the great Saint Pierre fish (more widely known as John Dory), served *au naturel* with anchovy butter – one of the stars of any menu. The other *pièce de résistance* that James and Patricia cooked and served each day was the freshest seafood chowder that money could buy, the ingredients garnered from the fishing boats berthed literally just a stone's throw away.

James would regularly take me across to the pier for the auctions when the fishing boats docked after several days at sea. There would be a huge array of seafood on view and, depending on the tides, the haggling could take place at any hour of the day or night, when sane people would be snug in their beds.

I have travelled to fish auctions and markets throughout the world since then, including: Billingsgate in London; Rungis market in Paris; the Gulf of Morbihan in Brittany; Spanish markets in search of prawns for *tapas gambas*; and the Florida Keys markets and Bahamian auctions in search of dorado, black grouper, barracuda and Chilean sea bass, to cook on board luxury cruise liners. I have trawled the markets of Maine looking for lobsters, spider crabs and soft-shell crabs for some of America's finest dining tables. But none of these compared at all to what was caught and sold in Greencastle on my own doorstep. This has had a lasting effect on me. I am in no doubt that this is the home of the best seafood in the world!

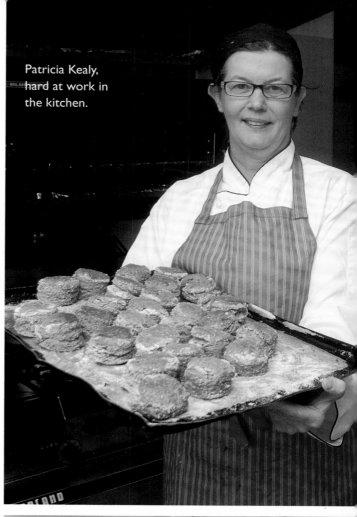

Patricia Kealy, hard at work in the kitchen.

James Kealy's Greencastle Chowder

Ingredients (Serves 6)

Greencastle Chowder
200g leeks, washed and diced
200g carrots, peeled and diced
200g onion, chopped
200g celery, chopped
200g potato, peeled, chopped and diced
50g butter
10g garlic, chopped
500g raw fresh seafood, diced (eg white fish, salmon, prawns, mussels etc)
600ml milk
1 litre fresh fish stock
50g plain flour or corn flour
10g pink peppercorns
10g fresh dill, chopped
75ml cream, crème fraiche (or natural yogurt)

Fresh Fish Stock (Fumet de Poisson)
1kg white fish bones
2 white onions, peeled and chopped
2 leeks, washed, peeled and chopped
100g unsalted butter
1 bottle dry white wine and 1 litre of cold water

Method

For the Fish Stock
1. In a heavy-based saucepan, sweat without colour the white fish bones in butter.
2. Add the chopped onions and leeks. Sweat for a further 5 minutes.
3. Add the water and white wine.
4. Bring to the boil and simmer for 20 minutes.
5. Pass through a fine sieve and leave to cool.

For the Chowder
1. Add butter to a heavy-based pan and, over low heat, sweat all the vegetables, without adding colour.
2. Add flour and mix until sandy texture is achieved.
3. Add fresh fish stock and milk slowly, stirring as you go.
4. Add pink peppercorns and chopped dill.
5. Bring to the boil slowly and simmer for 30 minutes. Finish with cream.
6. Add fresh seafood and shellfish and simmer for 5 minutes before serving.

Dancing with the Stars

Many world-renowned people have eaten at Kealy's and lavished praise on the food there. Nobel Laureate John Hume was a regular customer and brought important guests such as Irish president Mary Robinson, top international investors and US senator Ted Kennedy. I later heard that lots of the country's political agreements and business deals were struck here.

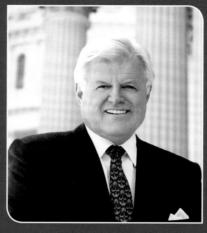

Senator Ted Kennedy

Playwright Brian Friel (below) was another patron, and his connection with the restaurant led to us catering one of the most spectacular events ever witnessed along the Foyle in 1991. A week prior to it happening, James Kealy announced to the staff that we would be preparing the finest buffet ever cooked; it was for a very special occasion and we were to pay huge attention to detail.

No-one asked who the buffet was for; it was all very hush-hush. But when the last finishing touches were being made to the Salmon Bellevue and the final ice sculptures had been shined and put into place, I was asked to accompany James to the buffet and serve the food.

'Look out for the wooden sign

between Greencastle and Moville reading "Dancing at Lughnasa",' Patricia explained to me as we were leaving. But this still didn't mean anything to me. So we turned left at the wooden sign and drove down a winding lane, which opened out to the most beautiful view of Lough Foyle and the Atlantic Ocean I had ever set eyes on. When we arrived, I was introduced to John Hume, Brian Friel and several famous actresses and actors.

After the buffet was served, I was to accompany Pat and John Hume by car to the pier at Greencastle and then on to Kealy's. As we approached the pier, I could see a large white yacht with a Tricolour rippling from its mast. John Hume stepped out of the car and boarded the yacht. Five minutes later, Taoiseach Charles Haughey, premier of Ireland, emerged from the cabin and greeted us.

Brian Friel's *Dancing at Lughnasa*, one of the great Irish plays of the 20th century, had opened on Broadway in New York that night. Ireland's leading statesmen, writers and actors had all gathered in Greencastle to celebrate with Kealy's finest food. And I had been fortunate enough to share that experience with them – all thanks to James and Patricia Kealy.

Brian Friel

John Hume

180

Amazing Swilly

Lough Swilly in the 18th century was a world-renowned fishing centre and historically significant in other areas, too. In 1748, the slaver John Newton experienced an epiphany there after finding safe harbour during a vicious storm. Newton went on to write the hymn *Amazing Grace* about his experiences. And Irish revolutionary Wolfe Tone was captured there in 1798.

To ?

How rare the scented air
Of this heather-covered hill
Where wild game, hares
And brockies roam at will

The tang of the Swilly dark
The smell of new-dug peat
Mingle to the music of the larks
To quiet minds a heavenly retreat

But all in all with nature that I am
I sometimes think she only works a charm
To thrill me with her moods and warm beams
These always fade and leave one only dreams

But you, my dear, whose love is always warm
Shall forever be when nature fails to charm.

Shaun McCourt, circa 1950s.

Moville, County Donegal.

MARKETS AND FAIRS.

WEEKLY MARKETS
Will be held EVERY THURSDAY in the Year, as usual.

MONTHLY FAIRS,
The LAST THURSDAY of every Month throughout the Year, for the Sale of HORSES, CATTLE, SHEEP, and PIGS.

In case Christmas Day should at any time fall upon the last Thursday in December, the Market and Fair will be held THE DAY BEFORE.

(By Order of the Patentee of the Moville Markets and Fairs.)

Market Square, Moville, County Donegal.

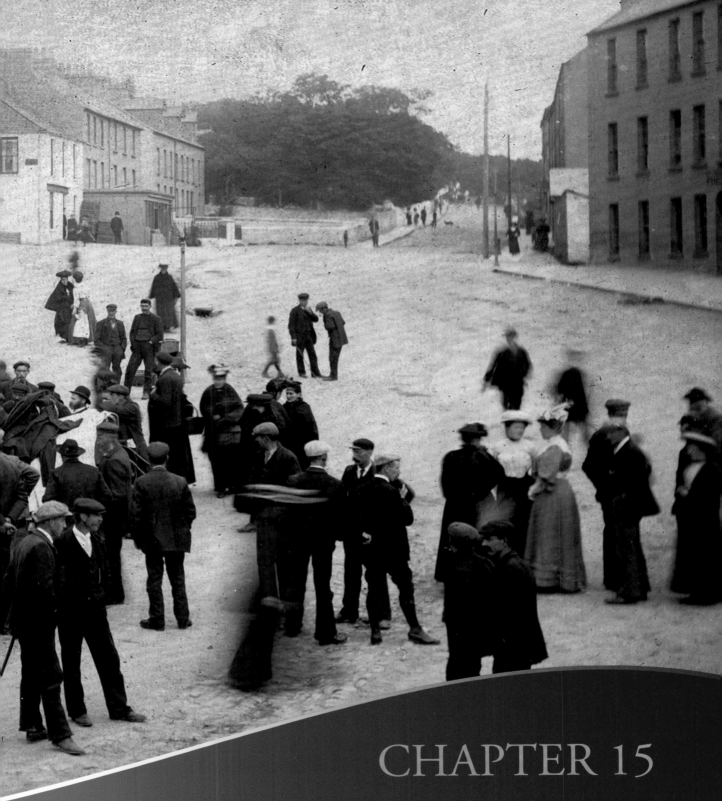

CHAPTER 15

Inishowen Culinary Tour Part I:
Greencastle – Rathmullan

ATLANTIC OCEAN

Map charting the three-stage culinary tour of Inishowen and NE Donegal.

LOUGH SWILLY

Malin Head

Culdaff

Carndonagh

INISHOWEN

Moville

Greencastle

CAR FERRY

Benone

Redcastle

LOUGH FOYLE

Buncrana

Fahan

CAR FERRY

Rathmullen

DONEGAL

Inch

Muff

Burt

Bridgend

Grianan

Derry

DERRY

N

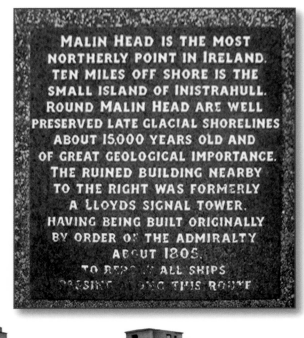

MALIN HEAD IS THE MOST
NORTHERLY POINT IN IRELAND.
TEN MILES OFF SHORE IS THE
SMALL ISLAND OF INISTRAHULL.
ROUND MALIN HEAD ARE WELL
PRESERVED LATE GLACIAL SHORELINES
ABOUT 15,000 YEARS OLD AND
OF GREAT GEOLOGICAL IMPORTANCE.
THE RUINED BUILDING NEARBY
TO THE RIGHT WAS FORMERLY
A LLOYDS SIGNAL TOWER.
HAVING BEING BUILT ORIGINALLY
BY ORDER OF THE ADMIRALTY
ABOUT 1805.
TO REPORT ALL SHIPS
PASSING ALONG THIS ROUTE

Malin Head signal tower
overlooking the North
Atlantic – next stop Iceland!

Greencastle and its near neighbour in County Donegal, **Moville**, are known the world over for the quality of their seafood. But other Inishowen towns and villages have also acquired prominent culinary reputations.

Several miles north of **Greencastle** is the small village of **Culdaff** which features **McGrory's** legendary Backroom Bar. The establishment is home to great food and also to some of the greatest gigs on the island, from Horslips to the Henry Girls. Indeed, it was selected as the IMRO Live Music Venue of the Year for 2012.

Next on our anticlockwise trip around the peninsula is **Malin Head**, a small fishing village sited on the most northerly (and possibly the most windswept) outpost in Ireland. Its pier was built in 1884 to receive cargo ships, but the seafaring traditions here date back to time immemorial. And for generations, hardy fishermen would have launched their boats from the beach into the mountainous seas that constantly thrashed the coastline before the pier was ever built.

Malin Head is one of the great crab-fishing centres of Europe, and the crab meat cooked here is the sweetest to be had anywhere. It is also home to fine oyster farms, including one operated by my childhood friend Jim Ball. He told me:

Before I set up in oyster farming I was a commercial fisherman. But fishing was on the decline and poor market prices for crab and lobster, along with the drop in salmon fishing, prompted me to reconsider my career although I still wanted to do something on the sea. At the moment, things are looking up. The Japanese and Chinese markets are buying a lot of oysters, which, along with the French market, may keep the demand for this shellfish going for years to come.

A few miles inland of Malin Head, and the town of **Carndonagh**'s once-famous market is today staging a major revival. Growers of the finest vegetables and makers of the finest home-cooked produce to be had can be found selling their wares every Saturday at Colgan Hall. The market hosts the talents of both local and international craftsmen. You will discover cheeses there to rival anything you would find in France. And the market's fresh breads and pastries could grace a top Parisian *boulangerie*, all made by Pâtisserie de Pascal.

About 12 miles southwest of Carn, on the Lough Swilly shore, lies the town of **Buncrana**, ancestral home of the North West's most prominent family – the O'Doherty clan. Buncrana was a hub for the Lough Swilly railway, and the old station house has been rein-

McGrory's of Culdaff.

The Drift Inn, Buncrana.

vented as the much-acclaimed **Drift Inn Bar & Restaurant**. The Drift is today renowned throughout the land for its 'doorstep' beef-and-onion sandwiches.

Another Buncrana restaurant well worth a visit is **The Beach House**, close to the pier, which is owned by Claire McGowan from Fahan. Claire uses as much local produce as possible in her establishment, from the fish of Greencastle to dry-aged Donegal beef, to Buncrana honey and carrageen moss. Buncrana is also home to one of the most fertile salmon rivers in the North West, the Crana.

If you've got a few hours to spare, depending on the season, you can take a five-mile ferry ride across the Swilly from Buncrana to **Rathmullan** village. Food lovers should be sure to visit **Rathmullan House Hotel**, which is just a two-minute walk from the pier. Owned by the Wheeler family since 1962, it is surrounded by award-winning gardens, which stretch down to the lough. There, the owners grow a wide range of vegetables and herbs, which are used in preparing the most sublime meals in their kitchen. A house speciality is the local favourite, carrageen moss.

The Beach House, Buncrana.

Above: Crana Bridge; good fishing can be found in these waters.
Below: Rathmullan House surrounded by its award-winning gardens.

Emmett's Potted Trout

Ingredients (Serves 6)

1.4kg trout/char cooked, skinned and boned
200g salted butter
½ clove of garlic, puréed
finely grated zest of 1 lemon
1 tsp of thyme picked, finely chopped
1 tsp of fresh fennel herb or dill, finely chopped
1 pinch of chilli
1 pinch of mace (nutmeg)
a small bunch of chopped chives
salt and pepper to season

Method

1. Cook the trout by panfrying or poaching and leave to cool.

2. In a heavy-based pan, on a very low heat, melt the butter until the white milk solids drop to the bottom of the golden clarified butter.

3. Skim off any white, foamy solids from the top of the butter. Add the garlic, lemon zest and herbs and take the pan off the heat. Add the spices and stir.

4. In a bowl, add the cooked, skinned and boned trout, flaking the flesh with a fork or by hand and removing any bones. Add chives and most of the clarified flavoured butter, retaining some for the end. Mix well and season to taste.

5. Pack into ramekins or sealed kilner jars, pressing down well. Top with remaining clarified butter and seal lid. This will keep up to two weeks in the fridge unopened. Once open, consume within 2 days.

6. Serve with wheaten bread or toast.

Malin Head Crab Cakes with Dulse and Lemon Mayonnaise

Ingredients (Serves 4)

Crab Cakes
300g white crab meat, picked of shell
100g cooked mashed potato (well drained)
2 tbsp mayonnaise
1 tsp Dijon mustard
fresh chopped chives
1 pinch of chopped fresh chilli
a drop of lemon juice

Pane (Breadcrumb Coating)
250g plain flour
200g egg wash (eggs and milk mixed)
500g white breadcrumbs
salt and pepper to season

Dulse and Lemon Mayonnaise
100g dulse
a drop of lemon juice
200g mayonnaise
salt and pepper to season
chopped fresh fennel herb

Method
For the Crab Cakes
1. In a bowl, mix the crab meat, cooked mashed potato, mayonnaise, mustard and chopped chives.
2. Add chopped chilli, lemon juice and season with salt and pepper to taste.
3. Cover and leave bowl in fridge.
4. Meanwhile, prepare the pane by placing the flour, egg wash and breadcrumbs into 3 separate containers.
5. Remove the crab mix from the fridge and use a tablespoon to portion equal quantities.
6. Roll the portion of crab mix into the palm of your hands to form a ball.
7. Flatten each ball with a palette knife to form discs of approximately 5cm in diameter and 1.5cm thick.
8. Pass through the flour and then into the egg wash. Gently pass through the breadcrumbs and leave to set in the fridge before frying.
9. Deep fry until golden brown and finish in the oven at 180C/Gas 4 for a further 10 minutes, until piping hot throughout.
10. Serve with dulse and lemon mayonnaise

For the Dulse and Lemon Mayonnaise
1. Wash the dulse thoroughly in cold water.
2. Boil the dulse in water for 5 minutes to reconstitute, then drain well.
3. Allow the dulse to cool and chop finely.
4. Add this to the mayonnaise with chopped fennel and lemon juice and mix well.
5. Season with salt and pepper.

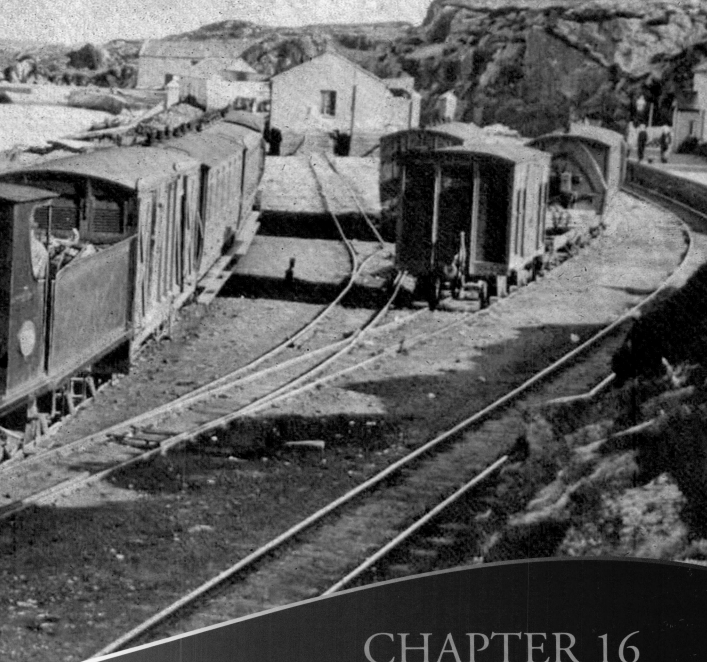

Lough Swilly Railway,
Fahan Station.

CHAPTER 16

Inishowen Culinary Tour Part II:
Buncrana – Inch

Continuing south from Buncrana towards Derry, you may be met at the roadside by fruit and vegetable sellers offering you excellent organic produce from the area. A word to the wise, don't be startled by the signs inviting you to sample the local Queens Big Balls of Flour – they are potatoes.

Next stop on our tour is **Fahan village**, site of the 7th-century abbey of St Mura, and latter-day home to Willie McCarter, who has been at the forefront of the North West whiskey revival. McCarter joined with his friend John Teeling, founder of Cooley Distillery in 1987, and revived the famous Derry-made brands of Tyrconnell and Inishowen.

'I returned from my studies in the US to Ireland in the early nineteen seventies to work in the family business in Buncrana,' explains McCarter. 'However, around this time the famous Derry distilling company Andrew A Watt, succeeded by Iriscot, went into liquidation, so I acquired the famous Watt brand names Tyrconnell and Inishowen. During the seventies and early eighties, I tried to revive these brand names but met with no success until John Teel-

> **Whiskey, Drink Divine!**
> Why should drivellers bore us
> With their praise of wine
> While we've thee before us?
> Whiskey, drink divine!
>
> (Joseph O'Leary, from *Ireland –
> The Taste and the Country*, by Mike
> Bunn, Gill & MacMillan, 1991)

ing formed Cooley Distillery at Riverstown on the Cooley Peninsula outside Dundalk. John then suggested I roll the brand names Tyrconnell and Inishowen into Cooley Distillery. Tyrconnell is now Cooley Distillery's leading single-malt brand and Inishowen is a very unusual Irish whiskey in that it is the only blended whiskey which contains a significant proportion of peated single malt.'

Cooley Distillery was acquired in 2011 by giant US spirits company Jim Beam who have begun to promote their Irish whiskey brands across markets worldwide.

Willie McCarter of Cooley Distillery.

Firebox Grill.

The Red Door, Fahan.

Just off the main road, as you descend to the new Fahan marina, you will find two fine restaurants just a stone's throw apart – both of which are historically quite significant. The **Railway Tavern & Firebox Grill** began life as the station house of the long-extinct Londonderry and Lough Swilly Railway Company. The restaurant, indeed, derives its name from the coal fireboxes in the locomotives, which were often used by engineers to cook themselves snacks. Refreshments have been provided for travellers here since the 1880s, instigated by innovative stationmaster James Bond, who also installed electricity at Fahan station many years before any of his competitors did so. The Railway Tavern became renowned as a first-class steak house under the stewardship of Ronan O'Heidin and Chris Furey. Be sure to check out their signature dish, 'Steak with Inishowen Whiskey'.

About 100 yards from The Railway Tavern is **The Red Door**, formerly known as Restaurant St John's (*not*, as legend had it, named after regular patron and Nobel Laureate John Hume). Local produce, including fish and seaweed, regularly feature on the menu here – and the views of Inch Island from the restaurant are spectacular.

The tranquil waters around Inch Island.

Specialities of the Firebox Grill, Fahan.

Surf and Turf.

Much of the land close to **Inch Island** and the nearby village of Burt was reclaimed from the sea in the 1850s and, as such, it is very flat and extremely fertile. The area was once home to one of Europe's great sea-trout fisheries prior to the decline in the industry in the 1980s. It also housed Ireland's largest dairy farm for many years.

Inch is where I first fished as a boy with my father, whose uncle Sean had a little cottage in the area. Farland Bank embankment separates a freshwater lake from Lough Swilly, and it was a great spot for catching white trout. We had some great catches there over the years. There is nothing as tasty as fresh white trout cooked in damp newspaper over the embers of a fire or fried in butter while out fishing.

The climate in this area is damp, but the land is free draining and enriched constantly with wind-borne deposits from the salty sea air. Thus it is used to grow barley, potatoes, turnips and rapeseed, and the yellow hue of rape can be seen carpeting the land in late spring. The pasture is also rich and is used to graze sheep and dairy cattle.

Lamb grazed here has a very special flavour and known all over the world. While training in France, I was amazed to learn that Salt-marsh Lamb, or Pre-Sale Lamb, was sought after all over the world by gastronomes and foodies.

And little did I know we have been producing this type of lamb for years, right on my very own doorstep!

Mill Bay, Inch Island.

Pot Roasted Pheasant with Bacon, Leeks and Carrots

Ingredients (Serves 4)

1 brace (2) of prepared oven-ready pheasants
6 slices of local streaky bacon
50g of butter
1 leek, washed and chopped
2 carrots, peeled and chopped
2 celery stalks, chopped
1 fresh bay leaf
1 sprig of thyme
1 sprig of rosemary
1 clove of garlic, peeled and roughly chopped
6 juniper berries
150ml of chicken stock
100ml of roast gravy (chicken, beef or game)
50ml dry white wine
salt and pepper to season

Method

1. Preheat the oven to 160C/Gas 3.

2. Cover each of the pheasants with 3 slices of streaky bacon.

3. Melt the butter in a heavy-based pot and add the vegetables, herbs and juniper berries. Sweat gently without colour for 10 minutes, turning regularly.

4. Place the pheasants on top of the vegetables, add the wine and garlic and simmer for 5 minutes on top of the stove. Add the stock.

5. Cover the pot with a lid and cook in the oven for 45 minutes. Add stock or water if required.

6. Take the lid off and put the pot back in the oven until the bacon is crispy, a further 10 minutes.

7. Take the pheasants out of the pot and keep warm (covered with tinfoil). Pick the herbs from the pot and reduce the cooking liquor by simmering. Add the roast gravy.

8. Serve whole or slice the breasts and legs away from the bird if desired.

Serve with boiled potatoes and ladle the vegetables and sauce from the pot over the pheasant.

Emmett's Game Pie

Ingredients (Serves 6)

200g rabbit leg or saddle, off the bone and diced
2 diced pheasant breasts
4 woodpigeon breasts, sealed (panfried on both
sides for 1 minute) and cut in two
2 woodcock or snipe breasts, sealed and cut in two
500g venison loin, diced
200g local streaky bacon, diced
300ml beef jus or chicken gravy
puff pastry sheets (enough to cover base and top of
pie dish)
egg wash (1 egg yolk mixed with a drop of water)
3 measures port
5 measures red wine
1 carrot, peeled and roughly chopped
1 medium onion, diced
2 cloves of garlic, chopped
1 tbsp juniper berries
fresh thyme, 1 small bunch, tied
Broighter Gold rapeseed oil for frying
salt and pepper to season

Method

1. Line a large pie dish with puff pastry and cut to size. Pin prick the base with a fork and set in fridge to rest.

2. In a heavy-based pot, add some rapeseed oil and sweat all the vegetables without adding colour.

3. Add all the game to pot, excluding the pigeon and woodcock.

4. When the game is sealed add port, red wine, gravy, thyme and juniper berries.

5. Bring to the boil and reduce the total volume by half by simmering.

6. Season with salt and pepper and add the sealed woodpigeon.

7. Allow to cool before filling the pie dishes with the filling.

8. Cut the puff pastry to fit the dish and cover the pie dish. Tie in the sides with a knife and brush the top with egg wash.

9. Preheat the oven to 180C/Gas 4. Cook for 30 to 40 minutes until golden brown. Serve with potatoes and vegetables in season. Also good served cold for lunch with crusty bread.

Scotch Boat Cranahan

Throughout the 19th and 20th centuries, many men left their homes in Derry, Greencastle and Magilligan and took the boat to Scotland to work on the pratie fields and farms as there was very little work in Ireland. As a result, great links were forged between Scotland and the North West over the years and a lot of Derry and Donegal families eventually settled in Scotland. Originally a celebration of harvest, there are many versions of this traditional Scottish pudding. Oatmeal is used again in this recipe as it was widely available. The fruits are bound with Scotch whisky.

Ingredients (Serves 4)

60g medium pinhead oatmeal or coarse oatmeal
150g summer fruits – raspberries, strawberries, blackcurrants etc
4 tbsp Scotch malt whisky
4 tbsp runny Scottish honey
600ml double cream
40g soft brown sugar

Method

1. Scatter the oatmeal onto a baking tray and toast in a low oven or under the grill until it becomes golden brown.

2. Care must be taken because the oatmeal can quickly burn.

3. Toast the oatmeal with a half measure of sugar together to give a crunchy texture and caramel flavour. This is done either under the grill or with care in a non-stick frying pan using a medium heat and tossing often.

4. Toss the summer fruits in whisky and warm honey.

5. Whip the cream, add the toasted oatmeal and then mix with the summer fruits, whisky and honey.

6. Spoon into glasses and drizzle some warmed whisky and honey over the cranahan.

An enthusiastic gathering celebrates the Dawn Chorus at Grianan of Aileach in 2013.

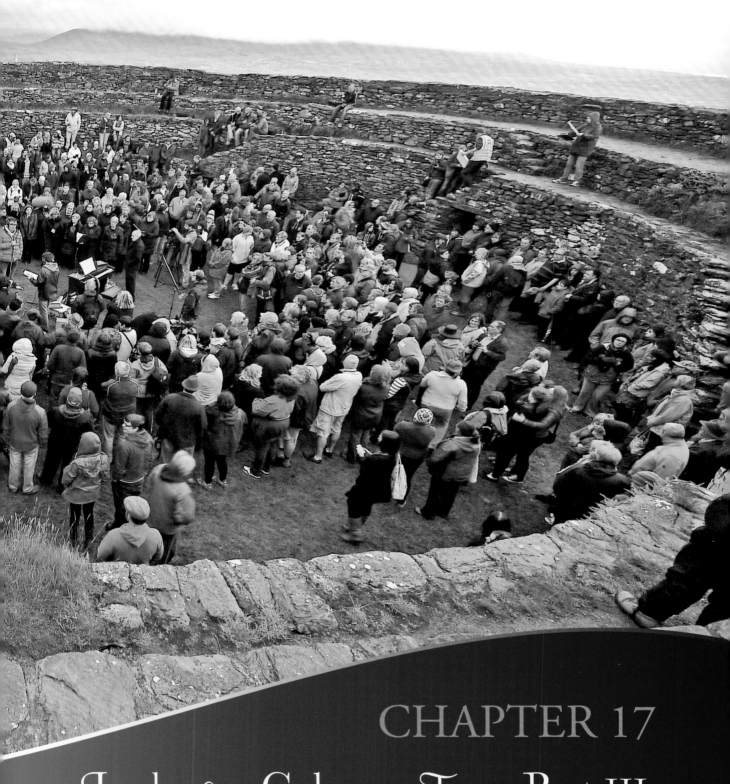

CHAPTER 17

Inishowen Culinary Tour Part III:
Burt – Redcastle

On the hilltop overlooking **Burt village** in County Donegal is one of Ireland's most famous landmarks, **Grianan of Aileach**. A round, stone fort, thought to have been constructed by High Kings of Ireland in the 8th century, it sits 802 feet above sea level and has the most breathtaking, panoramic views of Inishowen, Lough Swilly, Derry and Lough Foyle. Today, at the bottom of the hill is situated an interpretative hotel, **An Grianan**, built in honour of the ancient fort, where you will find fine food and hospitality.

Three miles away, close to the border leading back into Derry, is the village of **Bridgend**, which boasts one of the finest organic restaurants in the country, **Harry's**, run by Donal Doherty. Former chef Ray Moran and Donal won national acclaim for their use of the best of local produce, and the restaurant has been nominated as one of the 100 finest places to eat on the island.

On the little back road from Bridgend to **Muff**, which skirts Derry, you will find perhaps the finest selection of wild fruit and fungus in the country. In midsummer there's an explosion of colour, courtesy of berries like rose hip, gooseberries, blackcurrant, redcurrant, haws, and the Fraghan berry or bilberry. Later in the season you'll find crab apples, raspberries, blackberries and loganberries – a veritable forager's delight, particularly for jam-makers or winemakers. Mushrooms also abound, including the chanterelle and the wild cap.

This particular stretch of the North West countryside is a haven for wildfowl and game, furred and feathered. In early morning you will see rabbits and pheasants bursting from cover – or you might spot the zigzagging flight of the surprised snipe. Others to watch out for are mallard, widgeon and teal. A little further west you will find red deer grazing on corn and grass ripened by the unique moist climate.

It was on long walks through this countryside that my father passed on his love of the traditional, rural life to us. He taught us how to fish, hunt and catch rabbits – and he knew the name of every bush, flower and fruit along the hedgerows.

One man who knew this part of the countryside well was Jack Wallace. Jack grew up on the outskirts of Derry and recalled his experiences in the article 'Memories of an Outdoor Life' in the magazine *Waterside Voices*, 2011:

We always fished the Birdstown and Bridgend rivers towards the end of the season [September and October] when Dollagan trout, as we called them, would run up from Inch Lake. These are migratory brown trout with big red spots on both sides.

During the war [WWII], meat was very scarce in England, so rabbits were in great demand. Tony Coyle from Burt and his friend and neighbour Tommy McDermott, who lived about half a mile away, teamed up to go 'lamping' three or four nights a week, and they were making a fairly good living. Fowl dealers used to come round the farms every two or three weeks collecting unwanted hens, and they then came around every two or three days collecting rabbits. They paid one shilling and sixpence for each rabbit. It was said that in the West End of London, nineteen rabbits and one chicken in a large pot miraculously became twenty chickens …

One day, as I was in Foyle Street in Derry, I saw three fowl vans piled high with crates of rabbits awaiting their turn to load their cargo onto the Liverpool or Heysham boats. On a couple of the crates I noticed black wings sticking out and, on closer examination, discovered they were packed with crows. The driver said they were in great demand because of their white flesh and worth one shilling each. He didn't know what became of them on their arrival in England.

Rabbits were rampant in the North West in years gone by. Indeed, one gravestone at a Malin Head graveyard reads: 'Patrick Doherty, Father – Rabbit Catcher'. Across Lough Foyle at Magilligan there was one of the largest commercial rabbit warrens in Europe. Author and rabbit expert Steven McGonigal (left) recalled that the hatmakers from Strabane got first rights to the fur, but that there had to be referees on hand at the Magilligan rabbit fairs to stop fights over the price!

Magilligan even had its own special 'Grace Before Meals':

> *'For rabbits young and rabbits old/For rabbits hot and rabbits cold/For rabbits tender and rabbits tough/We thank you, Lord, we've had enough!'*

Between Bridgend and Muff we come to the townland of **Drumhaggard**, my father's birthplace. It borders Iskaheen which takes its name from the 'Pure Waters' (*Uisce Chaoin*) of a holy well of an ancient church which existed there.

Next stop is the village of **Muff**, home to two artisan butchers, **McColgan's** and **Lynch's**, both sellers of great meat products. McColgan's have some of the best lamb and beef available locally, while Lynch's homemade pork sausages are hard to beat.

North of Muff towards Moville, you will find some of the most beautiful views of Lough Foyle with no shortage of eating houses, restaurants and hotels, such as **The Redcastle Carlton** (Gordon Smith, chef), the **Ture Inn,** and **Mary Deeney's**. And all along the shore here you will see Lough Foyle lined with fishing boats and oyster and mussel fishers.

Immediately south of Muff, towards Derry, you will come to **Culmore**, formerly a fishing village and departure point for emigrants and now a rural suburb of Derry. Willie Lynch fished and picked periwinkles here for years before opening his own oyster farm, **Foylemore Oysters**. Also at Culmore you will find the **Magnet Bar**, incorporating Brown's Bistro, which boasts an award-winning menu.

Inishowen Rabbit with Dulse and Onion Poundies and Turnip Purée

Known as champ in other parts of Ireland, the word 'poundies' is particular to Derry and Donegal. This recipe is made with dulse, a great seaweed that is used widely in the North West.

Ingredients (Serves 2)

1 saddle of rabbit, boned out and trimmed (retain bones for sauce)
2 best end of rabbit, French trimmed
2 leg of rabbit – boned out (leg bone jointed, cut and retained for ballotine)
rabbit kidneys and livers
300g pork mince
200g chicken fillet, minced
150ml dry white wine
200g streaky bacon (Grant's)

1 clove garlic
100g chopped shallots
100g chopped scallions
10ml cognac
1 small bunch of fresh thyme
5g chopped fresh rosemary
250g chicken bones
50g tomato paste
2 litres water
300g mirepoix (roughly chopped carrot, onion, celery and leek)
300g turnip, trimmed and diced
20ml cream
200g potatoes, peeled and chopped
dulse, soaked and simmered in boiling water for 5 minutes
100g butter, diced

Method

For the Stuffing

1. Place the pork and chicken mince into a bowl, chop and add the rabbit liver and kidneys.

2. Sweat the shallots and garlic in butter with the chopped thyme and rosemary.

3. Add to the stuffing mix when cooled; mix and season. Add a little cracked egg to bind if necessary.

4. Fill a piping bag with the stuffing and leave to rest in the fridge.

For the Saddle

1. Lay the streaky bacon out on squares of tinfoil and clingfilm, place the saddle on top, season the inside of the saddle.

2. Pipe the stuffing inside the saddle, along the middle, and taking care not to overload.

3. Roll the foil slowly with the rabbit saddle turning both ends as you go to form a sausage shape. Tie both ends tightly and leave to set in fridge.

4. Place the saddle on a tray and roast in the oven at 180C/Gas 4 for 15 to 20 minutes. Allow to rest before carving.

For the Rabbit Ballotine

1. Proceed as for the rabbit saddle without the bacon, leaving a cleaned and chopped leg bone in the rabbit protruding from the top.

2. Pipe the stuffing along the inside. Roll as for the saddle. Leave to set in the fridge.

3. Braise in stock until cooked, (10 minutes).

For the Sauce

1. Roast the bones until well coloured in the oven, deglaze with the brandy.

2. Add the water. Brown the mirepoix of leeks, carrots, celery and onions in a frying pan.

3. Add all ingredients to a heavy-based sauce pan and bring to the boil, simmer for 3 hours skimming occasionally.

4. Pass through a fine sieve and reduce by half by simmering.

5. Add a small knob of butter before serving.

For the Turnip Purée

1. Braise the diced turnip in chicken stock until tender.

2. Purée turnip in blender and pass through a fine sieve.

3. Add a knob of butter and chopped rosemary when reheating.

4. Season to taste.

For the Poundies

1. Boil potatoes until tender, drain and mash.

2. Add the butter, milk, chopped cooked dulse and chopped onions.

3. Season to taste.

Poached Saddle of Rabbit with Armagh Apple Cider and Summer Flowers

Ingredients (Serves 2)

1 saddle of rabbit, boned out and trimmed
2 best end of rabbit (loin), French trimmed
2 rabbit legs, trimmed around the bone
300g pork mince
200g chicken fillet minced
150ml Carson's Crisp Armagh Apple Cider
200g local dry cured ham or streaky bacon
1 clove garlic
½ medium onion, roughly chopped
¼ diced onion for the stuffing
2 small bunches of fresh thyme
1 chopped fennel bulb
2 star anise
2 litres chicken stock
200g carrot, roughly chopped for garnish
300g turnip, diced for garnish
edible flowers – pea, chive, primrose, pansy, fennel
Broighter Gold rapeseed oil for frying
salt and pepper to season

Method
For the Stuffing

1. Place the pork and chicken mince into a bowl.

2. Sweat the diced onion and garlic in butter with the chopped thyme.

3. Add to the stuffing when cooled.

4. Mix and season. Add a little cracked egg to bind if necessary.

For the Saddle

1. Lay the cured ham or streaky bacon out on squares of good quality clingfilm, place the saddle on top, season the inside of the saddle.

2. Fill enough of the stuffing inside the saddle, along the middle as not to overload.

3. Roll the clingfilm slowly with the rabbit saddle, turning both ends as you go, to form a sausage shape. Tie both ends tightly. Leave to set in fridge.

4. To poach: Place the roughly chopped vegetables, herbs, star anise, stock and Carson's Crisp Armagh Apple Cider in a saucepan.

5. Place the saddle of rabbit, still wrapped in clingfilm, into the cooking liquor.

6. Bring to the boil and poach the saddle of rabbit for 10-15 minutes.

7. Allow to rest and remove clingfilm before carving.

8. Retain the cooking liquor to make the sauce.

For the Best End of Rabbit and the Legs

1. Preheat the oven to 180C/Gas 4.

2. Season the best end of rabbit and legs and fry in Broighter Gold rapeseed oil until browned.

3. Roast in the oven for 10 minutes.

4. Allow to rest before serving.

To Serve

1. Slice the saddle and place on a plate with the carrot and turnip garnish.

2. Reduce the cooking liquor by simmering, pass through a sieve and pour some over the saddle.

3. Place the cooked best end and leg on the plate and garnish with edible flowers. Serve with Carson's Crisp Armagh Cider.

Danger: Bootlegger at Work

Many years ago my father taught me how to make sloe juice and sloe gin, a great winter warmer for Christmas visitors. But rather than write down the recipe, I relied on his instruction, which was great, until one year he had a bad stroke and wasn't able to communicate the finer points to me as before. Regardless, I made up a batch of sloe juice and stored it in bottles in my lovely glass cabinet and left it to settle, confident I knew what I was doing.

One Friday night, after a long week at work, I had just put my feet up for a glass of wine with my partner Mary when an almighty explosion rocked the house. The bottles had exploded inside the glass cabinet!

When my father recovered from the stroke, he explained that he always buried the bottles in the garden, as they could explode if the tops were not loosened every so often. He added that the best method by far was to bury them in compost, as they would ferment quicker and you would obtain a more potent drink.

Sloes fermenting in a gallon bottle with demerara sugar added for sweetness.

Sloe Juice

Ingredients (1 bottle)

500g sloes
1 litre cold water
250g sugar

Method

1. Wash sloes thoroughly in cold water, removing any blackthorn leaves.

2. Place sloes and all other ingredients in plastic screw-top bottles.

3. Store in a warm dry place for up to 3 months or longer.

4. Release the screw tops slowly every couple of weeks and tighten again.

5. Store until required.

6. After 3 months, unscrew the bottles slowly and pass through sieve into clean bottles.

Emmett's Sloe Gin

Ingredients (1 bottle)

1kg sloes
200g granulated white sugar
1 bottle good quality gin

Method

1. Gather the sloes after the first frosts of the year (or else freeze before use) which has the same effect as cracking the skin of the berries.
2. Thoroughly wash the sloes in cold water, removing any leaves gathered.
3. Prick the sloes or store in bags in the freezer ready to be made.
4. Place washed sloes in plastic bottles, add the sugar and then the gin.
5. Store the bottles in a dry area for up to 3 months or longer, agitating the bottles every few days to disperse the sugar and mix the contents.
6. After 3 months, the sloe gin should have taken on a dark-claret red colour.
7. Pass into a bucket through muslin cloth or coffee filters to retain the berries and any sediment.
8. Adjust the flavour at this stage (if you need more sugar, or if not strong enough, add a few drops of gin). Then funnel into clean bottles.
9. Best served young at the festive season with ice or will mature if cellared for several years.

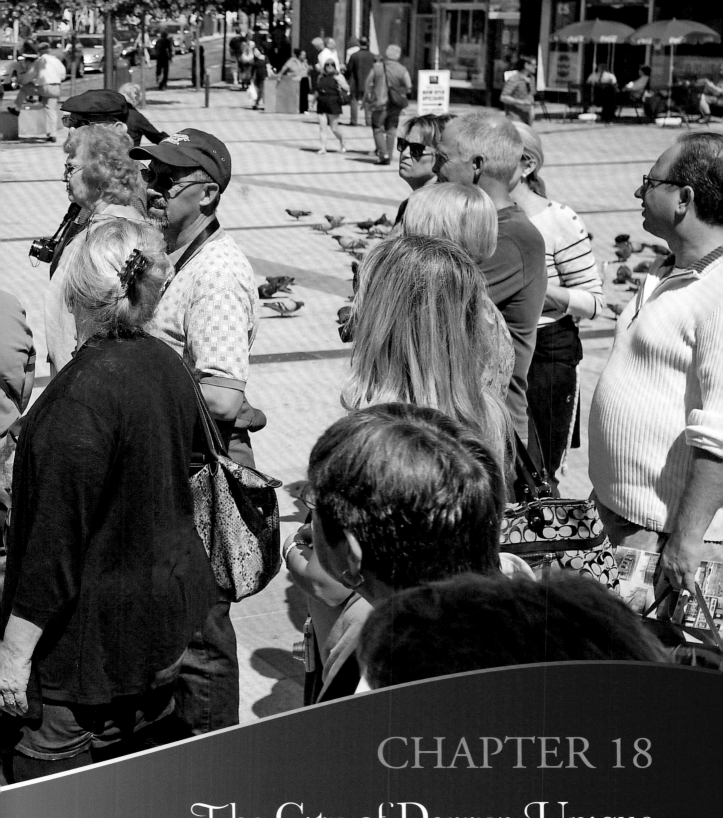

CHAPTER 18
The City of Derry's Unique Culinary Adventure

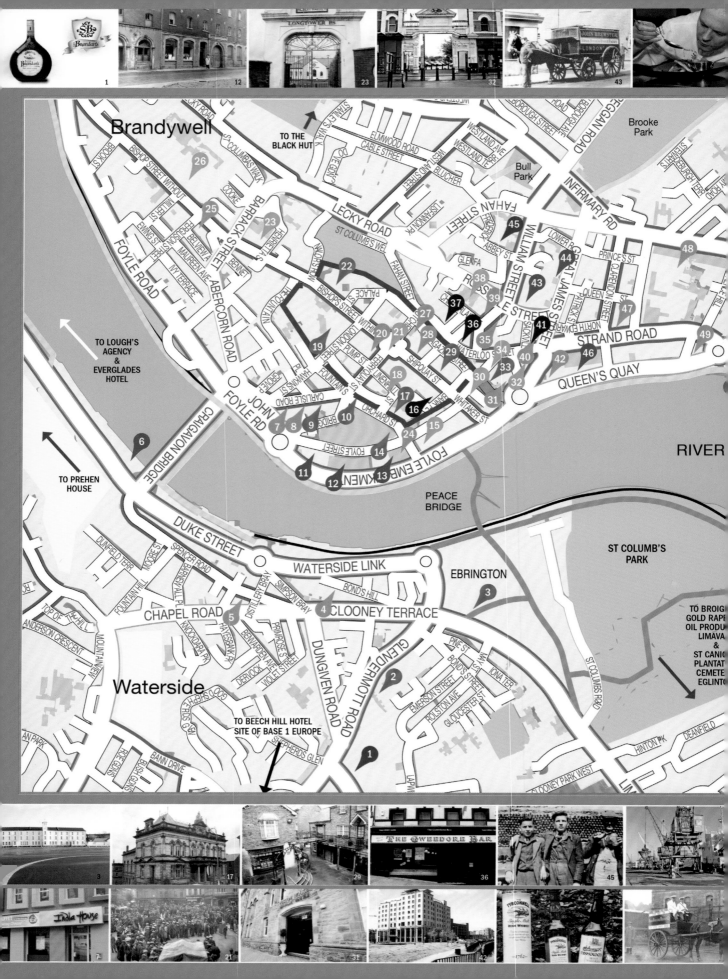

Brandywell

TO THE
BLACK HUT

Brooke
Park

Bull
Park

LECKY ROAD

26

25

23

22

FOYLE ROAD

TO LOUGH'S
AGENCY
&
EVERGLADES
HOTEL

6

TO PREHEN
HOUSE

JOHN
FOYLE RD

19

20 21

27

37

36

45

44

43

38

39

35

34

40

33

32

31

46

42

47

49

48

STRAND ROAD

QUEEN'S QUAY

INFIRMARY RD

41

30

28

29

18

17

16

7   8   9   10

11

12

13

14

15

24

RIVER

PEACE
BRIDGE

DUKE STREET

WATERSIDE LINK

CLOONEY TERRACE

EBRINGTON

3

ST COLUMB'S
PARK

4

CHAPEL ROAD

5

Waterside

2

TO BEECH HILL HOTEL
SITE OF BASE 1 EUROPE

1

TO BROIGH
GOLD RAPE
OIL PRODU
LIMAVA
&
ST CANIC
PLANTAT
CEMETE
EGLINTO

DUNGIVEN ROAD

THE GWEEDORE BAR

India House

TYRCONNELL

FOOD HERITAGE HOTSPOTS

RESTAURANTS / CAFES / SHOPS / HOTELS

FOOD PRODUCER / FACTORY / WAREHOUSE

LOCATION OF PARTICULAR HERITAGE INTEREST

FOOD / CATTLE MARKET

PUB / BAR

DISTILLERY

TO FOYLE BRIDGE & BOOM HALL

STRAND ROAD

DUNCREGGAN ROAD

The historic city of Derry can provide food enthusiasts with a unique culinary adventure that complements the wonderful local food on offer in the Inishowen hinterland. In the summer of 2013, the Irish Food Heritage Project launched 'Feast or Famine Food Adventures', an exciting new food tour with the aim of showcasing the city's award-winning and innovative restaurants and the quality of their heritage-related dishes.

I took several dozen visitors on guided walking tours of a range of Derry's first-class eating establishments, where they met the chefs and sampled locally sourced (and produced) food and drink while I recounted the story behind the city's fascinating food heritage. The response was amazing, and the tours are now a firm favourite in the summer calendar for visitors to our cultural city.

One of the main aims of the Irish Food Heritage Project is to promote the hard work, innovation and culinary expertise of the hospitality industry in Derry and the North West. I, therefore, include here some brief information on a cross-section of those restaurants, eateries, businesses and individuals who are contributing so much to either the

Food Adventure tour or the wider promotion of the city's culinary experience. This is by no means a comprehensive listing of all the food establishments in Derry. For that I can recommend the excellent *LegenDerry Food Guide* produced by Derry City Council in 2013 and which is available online at www.derrycity. gov.uk/legenderryfood.

I was lucky to learn my trade with several of the chefs listed below in my formative years as a young apprentice. And I am proud to note the number of my own former students, graduates of the School of Hospitality at the NW Regional College, who now work alongside these chefs and are making their own personal contributions to the hospitality industry across the North West.

Ardmore at Beech Hill Country House Hotel
Ardmore, Waterside
Barry O'Brien, Chef

This is one of the establishments where I first honed my culinary skills under the leadership of then chef Noel McMeel. Patron Patsy O'Kane has always run one of Ireland's finest dining and hospitality experiences, catering to presidents and dignitaries from across the world. Chef Barry O'Brien and his talented young team create an array of dishes of great quality and artistic inventiveness.

Belfray Country Inn
Glenshane Road, Waterside
Charlie Dillon, Chef

I trained at Portrush Catering College with Charlie Dillon who leads the team at The Belfray. One of his signature dishes is herb-crusted fillet of salmon served with creamed cabbage and smoked pancetta.

Brown's Restaurant
Bond's Hill, Waterside
Ian Orr, Chef, and Marcus Roulston, Patron

Ian Orr (bottom left) is one of Ireland's most talented chefs. Ian won the Georgina Campbell Irish Chef of the Year Award in 2013, was a finalist in the BBC Great British Menu in 2012 and became a brand ambassador for Lidl in 2013. Ian is renowned for his dedication to seasonal produce from local suppliers.

Speciality/signature dish: Atlantic pan-fried scallops with braised pork cheeks from local butchers, star anise and delicious apple purée.

Brown's in Town
Strand Road
This sister restaurant of chef Ian Orr's Bond's Hill premises serves contemporary fine dining in fashionable city-centre surroundings.

Signature dishes include Brown's style chicken and chorizo sausage roll for lunch; and pan-seared scallops, prawn tortellini, and pork and bacon ragout for the evening menu.

Custom House Restaurant
Queen's Quay
Chris Moran, Chef
This restaurant is situated in the former 19th-century Custom House, where emigrants signed off to leave on the famine ships. Chef Chris Moran and his team lead this luxurious restaurant and wine bar.

Chris's signature dish is salt-and-chilli squid served with pak choi, peppers and dips, consisting of sweet chilli, wasabi mayonnaise, soy and ginger.

The Delacroix Restaurant
Buncrana Road
This long-established eatery lies at the gateway to Donegal and offers a friendly, modern dining experience. They pride themselves on their locally sourced meats and fish and one of their most popular dishes is fillet steak Lyonnaise topped with Cashel Blue cheese.

The Exchange Restaurant
Queen's Quay
Mark Caithness, Chef/Patron
Situated in the old telephone exchange building and next to the former Goose Market, The Exchange has established itself as one of Derry's most visited eating institutions. One of their signature dishes is the popular, locally sourced crispy duckling, complete with caramelised skin and tender meat, accompanied by a caramelised orange sauce.

Encore Brasserie
Millennium Forum, Newmarket Street
John McGee, Chef
This modern brasserie is located in the lobby of Derry's state of-the-art theatre. Charis Jones, Manager, and Chef John McGee believe in using only locally sourced ingredients. Speciality/signature dishes: Dexter beefburger and home-cut chips for lunch; crispy pork on the bone served with sauté savoy and roasting jus for that fine evening dining experience.

221

Brown's

Brown's

Custom House

Custom House

Encore Brasserie

Fitzroy's

The Exchange

The Exchange

Everglades, the Grill
Prehen Road
Colman O'Driscoll, Executive Head Chef
The Everglades Hotel was one of the first restaurants I worked in. I trained under Terry Francis and Peter Lafferty, two great chefs who put me in the care of Micky McCay and Mark O'Hare (chef de parties at the time). Mickey challenged me every day by selecting different potato dishes from the *Repertoire de la Cuisine* (the chef's bible) to cook for the staff. As a result, I knew all the classical potato dishes by the time I left the Everglades Hotel and Portrush Catering College.

Speciality/signature dish: Guinness-battered scampi made from deliciously fresh and succulent langoustines, which are landed in Kilkeel Harbour, County Down.

Fitzroy's
Carlisle Road
Ruairi Gallagher, Chef
Situated just outside the city's historic walls, Fitzroy's has been a local institution for over fifteen years. Chef Ruairi Gallagher is an ex-student of mine and has been leading the kitchen team at Fitzroy's for the past number of years. Speciality/signature dishes: Cajun chicken with goat cheese and vegetable stir-fry; chilli and ginger chicken; and herb-crusted pork fillet with Clonakilty black pudding and vanilla/parsnip purée.

La Sosta Ristorante
Carlisle Road
Claudio and Maureen Antonucci, Owners
Established in 1995, La Sosta is an atmospheric Italian family restaurant. It offers an authentic taste of Italy providing light, modern cuisine using the best of local, seasonal ingredients, with the emphasis on quality and detail. Their speciality is fillet steak with porcini mushrooms, truffle and Grand Marnier sauce.

La Sosta

The Metro Bar
Bank Place
Kieran Dunne, Chef

The restaurant here is owned and operated by my good friend Kieran Dunne. The Metro is one of the most popular city-centre spots and today is taking its rightful place in Derry's buzzing food scene offering an eclectic mix of Irish pub classics with international culinary favourites.

NWRC Flying Clipper Restaurant & Erin Room Brasserie
NW Regional College, Strand Road
Emmett McCourt, Chef & Lecturer

The North West Regional College boasts three fine eateries within the college: The Erin Room, Flying Clipper and Larry Hill.

These restaurants have become known locally for their five-star dining experiences with excellent cuisine and first-class service. All NWRC eateries offer the public value for money, and a customer focus you will only find at the very best hotels.

The excellent and award-winning hospitality staff, who have cooked in some of the finest kitchens worldwide, transfer and impart their skills on a daily basis to local and international students. This is where you will find me throughout the year, cooking with students and staff for the general public.

The restaurants at NWRC also boost a real food heritage story as two of them are named after famine ships owned by the locally based McCorkell Line – *The Erin* and *The Flying Clipper*.

The Metro

224

Flying Clipper
NWRC RESTAURANT

north west
regional college
Derry~Londonderry • Limavady • Strabane

The kitchen of the old Technical College (Lawrence building), 1905.

Quay West

Quay West

Quay West

Darren Iddon,
Queen's Quay Social

Da Vinci's

Da Vinci's

Pyke 'N' Pommes
Street Food

Kevin Pyke's hugely popular mobile catering venture is located on the quay close to Baronet Street. This is a truly different dining experience, delivering restaurant standard food at street food prices. From slow-cooked shoulder of pork to the famous 'Codfather', Pyke 'N' Pommes rivals any of the increasingly popular, and highly fashionable, pop-up street-food eateries to be found in major cities throughout the world such as Lucky Chips in London.

Kevin's other signature dish is the 'Notorious PIG' Wrap, slow-cooked shoulder of pork, with homemade crispy slaw and smoked BBQ sauce, all wrapped in Lebanese flatbread.

Quay West
Boating Club Lane
Gareth Ferry, Patron

Situated on Queen's Quay, in the 19th-century former boathouse for the City of Derry Rowing Club, overlooking the beautiful River Foyle, Quay West has been serving up top quality food for manys a year under Gareth Ferry's fastidious leadership. It is said that the bell above this building was rung every time a famine/emigration ship left Derry port for the New World in the mid-19th century.

Queen's Quay Social
Queen's Quay
Darren Iddon, Chef

The 'social eating' concept was introduced to Derry by my good friend, Liverpool-born Chef Darren Iddon. Queen's Quay Social is a modern, contemporary eating-house with informal dining. Guests eat, drink and socialise together over everyday affairs or special occasions. The food and service at this venue, which lies at the heart of the city's 'Restaurant Quarter', are first class.

Ramada Da Vinci's Grill Room
Culmore Road
Declan Hutton, Head Chef

This well-established and popular restaurant changes its comprehensive menu seasonally, sourcing the finest local ingredients for the best in modern Irish cuisine. It also features a glass-sided wine room with the finest selection of vintages from around the world. Favourite dishes include the locally sourced 28-day, dry-aged steaks.

The Sooty Olive
Spencer Road
Sean Harrigan, Chef & Owner
Owner/chef Sean Harrigan and his team include first-class starters such as their flavoursome Asian squid topped with salt-and-chilli Asian stir-fry, served with a chilli and peanut dip. Main dishes include pan-seared local duck breast, served with braised red cabbage, carrot purée and spiced jus.

Thompson's Restaurant, City Hotel
Queen's Quay
Paul Sharkey, Executive Chef
Paul Sharkey's skilled team utilise quality local produce to prepare an extensive menu offering lots of choice at this sleek restaurant on the site of the imposing former Thompson's Mill that stood on the old city quay for decades. Signature dishes include crispy grilled fillet of Donegal hake served on a bed of creamy champ.

Timber Quay Restaurant
Strand Road
Colin Harrigan, Chef/Patron
Owner and Chef Colin 'Harry' Harrigan trained with me at the Everglades Hotel many moons ago! Harry works hard to ensure that all their food is locally sourced – especially for his TQ burger, which has become a firm favourite with his discerning customers.

Tower Hotel, The Walls Restaurant
Butcher Street
This contemporary and increasingly popular restaurant adjacent to Derry's historic City Walls is proud of its locally sourced seafood and beef. Even the bottled water served at the bars and restaurant is from the locale.

The Walls Restaurant's acclaimed signature dish is saddleback pork belly crackling, served with creamy Dauphinoise potatoes and cider jus.

White Horse Hotel
Campsie
Noel Ward, Executive Chef

The White Horse Hotel is nestled near the banks of the River Faughan, close to the ancestral home of the Gettys and to the Plantation Cemetery of St Canice's where some Getty family members are buried. The restaurant is headed by award-winning chef Noel Ward, an ex-student of NWRC.

Sooty Olive

Tower Hotel

City Hotel

A Different Culinary Experience

Derry and its environs also provide a wide range of multi-cultural casual eating experiences in restaurants, cafes, bistros, bars, coffee and teahouses etc. You will find snacks and specialty foods and drinks to satisfy all palates. Many of these eateries have won awards for their produce, service, culinary expertise or innovative methods, from a variety of prestigious professional and industry sources. These include:

Austins Rooftop Restaurant & Café Mezzo, The Diamond – located in Ireland's oldest department store Austins (see below right c.1900). The rooftop restaurant provides spectacular views of the city. Café Mezzo offers high-quality bistro eating at excellent rates.

Badger's Bar & Restaurant, Orchard Street – an award-winning bar and restaurant located between the two main shopping malls in the city Foyleside and the Richmond Centre.

Bloom's Café, (VAC), Stable Lane – situated within the historic Derry Walls and allowing passage directly onto the ramparts of the Walls.

The Buttery, Strand Road – opposite the old Victoria Market for a great cup of tea and buttered scone. Inspired by the city's rich heritage of city-centre tearooms.

Caife Fáilte, Cultúrlann Uí Chanáin, Great James Street – steeped in Irish culture and heritage with fine Irish cuisine, Caife Fáilte provides traditional Irish food with modern interpretations. Overseen by Manager Jim Hamilton, along with Marie Doherty and her team, the restaurant serves up traditional Irish stew and broths, heart-warming soups and delicious sandwiches. All the food is home cooked and locally sourced, with the bread coming from McDaid's Bakery, another one of Derry's family bakery institutions, which once occupied this site. McDaid's still run their popular business on the outskirts of the city selling some of the tastiest breads in the North West.

Café Del Mondo, Craft Village – this multicultural bistro offers everything from delicious dishes from around the world to stunning artisan breads baked on the premises as well as a variety of great lunch choices. The menu is shaped by talented young chef Stephen Forbes, who is as comfortable brewing a wild consommé with truffle foam as cooking fish, just hours out of the cold Atlantic, with clarified butter.

Café Soul, Shipquay Street – renowned for its homemade breakfasts and outside dining area. It also hosts regular entertainment evenings featuring top local talent.

Cedar, A Taste of Lebanon, Carlisle Road – for the true taste of the Middle East.

Fiorentini's, Strand Road – this nationally-renowned café is a cross-generational favourite of North West residents which celebrated its centenary in 2013. Fiorentini's is famous for its homemade ice cream and signature fish and chips.

Flaming Jacks, Strand Road – serves tasty, well-served food and was winner of Best Casual Dining, Derry, in 2012 (awarded by the Restaurant Association of Ireland).

Guild Café, Guildhall Square – a new addition to Derry's eating scene, set inside the city's landmark seat of local government, the Guildhall. The café is operated by Claire McGowan, who also runs the award-winning Beech House in Buncrana.

Café Soul

Guild Café

Kataya, Waterloo Place – there has been an upsurge in Kebab Houses and Middle Eastern eateries in Ireland in recent years. Kataya's homemade naan bread, made on site, is a perfect accompaniment to its fine Doner King.

Legenderry Warehouse No 1, Guildhall Street – featuring a bohemian/warehouse décor, and using recycled materials from local factories, this welcoming eatery offers a great menu – ranging from hearty breakfasts and sourdough sandwiches to heart-warming soups and salads. All vegetables and salads are grown in their own walled garden in County Donegal.

Mama Masala, Queen's Quay – the North West's only Indian Tandoori restaurant/Italian pizzeria!

Mandarin Palace/Karma Restaurant, Queen's Quay – offers many different styles of cooking from throughout Asia, including Szechuan, Canton and Malaysian.

Martha's Vineyard, Brunswick Cinebowl, Pennyburn – award-winning restaurant adjacent to a multi-cinema complex. Great for a family night out.

Molly's, Craft Village – named after the grandmother of owner, Gerard. Their delicious stew is home cooked and prepared using the freshest ingredients.

Paolo's Pizzas, Waterloo Street – for first-class pizzas in Derry since 1989, operated by Paul McShane and Eugene Bell.

Primrose Café, Carlisle Road – a new dining experience with great food.

The Sandwich Company, Strand Road, Bishop Street and four other locations – one of Derry's longest established cafés, the Sandwich Company offers the city's largest range of sandwich combinations at its six outlets, as well as salads, stews, soups and baked potatoes.

Artisan Producers, Suppliers, Butchers & Bakers

Doherty's Bakery

One of Derry's long-established culinary institutions and inventors of the famous Derry bap, Doherty's Bakery operate at three locations across the town – Foyle Street, William Street and Bishop Street. Doherty's is a family-run business, which has been serving the best of buns, breads and cakes to the city public for the last 80 years. Ciara Cassidy (née Doherty) manages the shops, while her baker brothers operate the factory/bakery in Pennyburn. Ciara's grandmother founded the bakery from her own kitchen, and the scone bread and Derry bap recipes, used by Mrs Doherty, are still in use today.

Donegal Prime Fish

Derry also boasts leading seafood suppliers and fishmongers Donegal Prime Fish at Skeoge Industrial Estate. The facility is owned by Dorothy Ryan and managed by Patsy Farren. I have been using Donegal Prime Fish for many years now as a chef, and the standard of their produce is first class. Furthermore, the variety of fish to be had from Donegal Prime has to be seen to be believed, and they will always try to source fish for you, travelling as far as London's famous Billingsgate market if they can't find it locally. When I was training as a chef at the Everglades, I remember owner Reggie Ryan's humble beginnings selling fish from his car. Donegal Prime Fish have grown from strength to strength over the years and they produce without doubt one of the best artisan smoked salmon brands from these islands, Irish Silver.

Gallagher's Butchers, William Street

Owned by Jack Doherty and managed by Gregory Doherty, their meat products are second to none. Gallagher's are also licensed game dealers and specialise in quality venison and rabbit. Their venison burgers in season are a perennial favourite. Gallagher's Butchers are also credited for producing the famous Derry rissole, made with minced pork and a special spice ingredient, which is then dipped in breadcrumbs and shallow-fried. Similar to the Belfast pasties, these rissoles have been popular with Derry people for decades. Dessie Begley (Master Butcher) will source most meat cuts for you, including pigs' trotters.

Harlequin's Bakery

Located at Ebrington Terrace in the Waterside, Harlequin's is owned by Michael Irving, a graduate of NWRC. It is a welcome addition to the artisan bakeries of the city. Michael sells a range of freshly baked heritage breads from his Waterside shop including Indian meal, oaten, Guinness and scone bread. Michael's bakery has become a popular spot for cupcakes, baked apple tarts and pastry products.

Paul's Butchers, Culmore Road

Paul's Butchers are renowned for their first-class food, service and value. Award-winning suppliers, they stock the best quality meats including beef, pork, lamb, fresh poultry, dry-aged steak and much more. They believe in the heritage method of maturing meat so they let it hang (dry-aged) for three to four weeks before using. As a result, the meat you purchase from Paul's Butchers will be incredibly tender and full of flavour. They pride themselves on their large selection of artisan-prepared ready-to-eat meals.

The Traditional Derry Chippy/Fishy

A food tour of Derry would not be complete without taking a look at our local fish and chip shops which created so many fond memories for generations of local families. The Italians were the first to sell fish and chips when they came to Derry at the start of the last century. But other Derry entrepreneurs started off selling fish and chips from their home kitchen (just as they had in previous generations with pigs' trotters). When my family moved to Carnhill at the start of the Troubles, the chip shop was a welcome treat on a Friday, due to the religious tradition of only eating fish, not meat, on a Friday.

I still recall going to Lexy's in Shantallow and the delicious taste of the homemade chips, cooked in lard, with lashings of salt and vinegar. Elsewhere in the city, Brennan's on Stanley's Walk were renowned far and wide, as were Gibbon's in Rosemount and Duddy's in the Glen. Frankie Ramsey's, now Café Grianan, in William Street was also a favourite for several generations of late-night revellers. It's great to see that tradition still being carried on today by many fine chippies across the city, including Bridie's (several outlets) and Terry Casson's Crescent Chippy.

Fish and chips first became available in Derry through Italian cafés like Yanarelli's on Strand Road,

A firm favourite among young people out enjoying a night on the town was Duddy's fish-and-chip shop on William Street.

Frankie Ramsey's on Willaim Street, pictured here in the early 1990s, was a fine example of a traditional Derry chippy.

Some celebrated regional produce: Doherty's Meats, Glens of Antrim Potatoes, St Brendan's Irish Cream Liqueur and Broighter Gold Rapeseed Oil.

CHAPTER 19

21st-Century World Beaters

DOHERTYS
Tradition of Quality

Eaton's

The Dohertys Team (L-R): Eibhlin Cassidy, Matthew Doherty (Director), James Doherty (Director), Treasa Harkin, Paul Hegarty (Sales Development Manager) and Brian McQuaid (Sales Manager).

As the 20th century wore on, many local food and drink providers – grocers, bakers, brewers, distillers and butchers – disappeared from the North West landscape, many of them unable to compete with the multinationals. Names like **Stevenson's**, founded in the 1840s as a 'fancy bread and biscuit bakery', and which later branched into confectionery, vanished into the ether, as did the multi-generational family firm **Brewster's**. Another great Derry bread-maker, Eaton's, amalgamated with Hughes Bakery in Belfast in the 1970s to become Peter Pan.

There will always be a demand for high-quality local produce, however, and some family firms thrived and acquired national, if not international, reputations. **Daniel Doherty Bakery** (Moville) and **William Grant & Co** (meat produce manufacturer), based in Culmore, are two exemplars of this.

Perhaps Derry's most famous, long-standing food institution has been **Doherty's Meats**. Founded by James Doherty in 1830, the business was continued by his son and grandson, and by 1945 comprised a small retail chain owned by Thomas J Doherty. In that year, the current chairman, James Doherty, joined his father and began a process of expansion and development into processed beef and pork products. The company's specialities today include 'special' mince, sausages and puddings. Doherty's is managed by James's sons, Seamus and Ian, and in 2010 the handover to a sixth generation began.

Doherty's have been strong performers in the export market, too. Since 2009 they have been supplying gluten-free sausages to 300 Asda stores in Britain. And in 2013 they secured a major new contract to supply 44 Scottish supermarkets with 'Superior Irish Pork Sausages'.

At a local and regional level, Doherty's Meats has, for generations, been synonymous with one of Derry's most cherished dishes – the Derry stew. A Derry stew is a simple, economical but truly tasty and filling meal. And at the heart of it will always be Doherty's mince. Like wine connoisseurs, a debate will always rage between the advocates of 'standard' and 'special' types of mince. But regardless of your choice – in homes across the North West – it has to be Doherty's.

A Derry Food Legend

My Doherty ancestors moved to Derry around the turn of the 1800s from Inishowen. My grandfather died in 1903 and my father took over the butcher's business which had three people working in it at the time. The first shop was on 36 Foyle Street opposite the Melville Hotel, long gone now. They also had premises in Great James Street and Waterloo Place. I started in the business part time in 1940 when I was only 16.

There were a lot of markets then: the cattle market, butter market, goose market etc. Derry seemed to have prospered because of the shirt industry which was also growing at the time. There was always a great sense of community in Derry back then.

The pork industry was widespread in Derry and beyond and there were people who made a fortune gathering brock for the pigs. Most people kept a pig back then and would have grown their own vegetables, too.

The war years were tough for butchers with a scarcity of meat and food in general; everything was rationed during the war. It was tough during those years, but I also saw potential in manufacturing.

Doherty's mince was really developed – and made famous I suppose – by my father who created a formula for it. He passed the spice mix on to me and we followed it rigidly.

My father had obviously caught the palate of the Derry people. It wasn't hit or miss, it was carefully worked out. There was a different spice for the mince than for the sausages, to really enhance the flavour of the mince. Basically, it's a simple enough process, but it calls for a strict attention to detail. It's this detail that produces a high-quality product that is hard to beat. I remember a chap coming to me once who had made a mistake with the mince formula. I told him to throw it all out. 'What! Throw it all out?' he said. 'Sure nobody would notice!' 'Yes, throw it out,' I said. That's how we maintain the quality!

We would go to great lengths to enhance and develop the quality of our products – even travelling to America to research new production methods. We had family in America who invited us out. I was actually anxious to go to the US as I was aware that a particular meat plant there had a machine that would have been very useful to us. My US relatives managed to get me into that plant. I knew that some of the techniques the Americans had in meat production were innovative. They were relatively simple but improved the quality of the output. We had our own techniques but we missed out on certain elements, and when I was in America I saw immediately where we

JAMES DOHERTY,
BUTCHER,
36, Foyle Street, Derry.
CORNED BEEF and PICKLED TONGUES always in Stock.
SAUSAGES and MINCED MEAT of Best Quality,
Fresh Daily
ORDERS PUNCTUALLY ATTENDED TO.
Terms Moderate.

could advance our own production methods, and this made all the difference.

Our mince is basically similar to the American version, such as Philadelphia-style mince or the kind that is used for Sloppy Joes. But their method is to produce it initially without flavour and then they add the flavour afterwards. Doherty's mince has the flavour built into the manufacturing process from the start. But there needs to be consistency and the right procedures have to be in place.

Mince was a great product that everybody took to. If you went along the Lecky Road in Derry at dinnertime on any day you would be sure that in practically every house there was a man cooking mince for his wife coming back from the shirt factory. It wouldn't all have been Doherty's mince they were cooking but we were the pioneers of it though. It was very economical to buy mince; a pound of mince would provide dinner for a whole family. The people of Derry were brought up on Doherty's mince and the women of Derry improvised meals with it.

I also travelled to Frankfurt with my friend John Sawyer from Belfast to examine how the Germans made their sausages. This helped us develop our black and white pudding and our own sausage brand. We also developed a great relationship over the years with William Grant's who were able to source the best cuts of pork for our sausages.

There were a lot of butchers in Derry at the time and Bishop Street and William Street housed many of them. There was Hutton's, Quigley's, Willie Gallagher's, and McCourt's on Waterloo Street. Gallagher's are still in William Street, but this is now owned by Jack Doherty's Butchers who kept Gallagher's name above the shop. Gregory Doherty, Jack's son, now manages the butchers.

It was a great way of life back then. It was amazing to see all the artisan products on display. It seems to be going back to those days

A true family enterprise: James and Matthew are the sons of Joint Managing Director Seamus Doherty. They are the sixth generation of Dohertys to be involved in the business.

again now. With all the recent food scandals, people need to know where their meat is coming from, so traceability is a big factor today in meat production. There are a lot of supermarket butchers about now, but they normally contain young staff with very little training. There's nothing that compares with going into a butcher that you know at the corner of the street who has expertise to share, and usually with a bit of banter. Your local butcher normally can give you good advice of how best to utilise the meat products.

The displays in the butchers' shop windows were something to see back then. My father developed a method of keeping the meat cool by having water constantly running down the shop window, which kept the meat at the proper temperature inside the shop.

We sold poultry at one stage, too, and had a rotisserie installed to cook the chickens. This was quite successful. Hegarty's butchers on William Street are still using a rotisserie to this day, and it seems to be quite popular.

We must be one of the oldest food businesses in Derry and have always had very good staff which has stood in our favour over the years. Two of the grandsons are working in the business now – James and Matthew – so I am hopeful they will help to maintain the legacy of Doherty's Meats well into the future.

Above: A very simple dish to prepare, Doherty's mince stew can feed a family for a couple of days and many believe it tastes even better the next day.

Right and below: Most families love their 'stews'. Wholesome and filling, the end result is always an empty plate!

Doherty's Mince Stew

Many generations of North West mammies and grannies have reared their families on Doherty's mince stew.

Ingredients (Serves 4)

500g Doherty's mince ('Standard' or 'Special') hand-rolled into balls
2 large carrots, peeled and chopped
2 onions, peeled and chopped
100g turnip chopped (optional)
1kg potatoes, peeled and chopped
175ml beef stock (optional)
1 litre water, just enough to cover ingredients
salt and pepper to season

Method

1. Place all vegetable ingredients in a heavy-based pan, add the Doherty's meatballs.

2. Barely cover with just enough stock or water.

3. Bring to the boil and simmer for 45 minutes to 1 hour or until the stew resembles a thick consistency, when the potatoes are cooked and well broken up.

4. Adjust the seasoning with salt and pepper.

5. Serve hot from the pot with Worcester Sauce (or brown or red sauce – the choice is yours!)

There has also been a considerable resurgence in Derry's drink-manufacturing industry over the past 30 years. Niche Drinks have capitalised on the North West's dairy industry to produce **St Brendan's**, a superior Irish Cream Liqueur. The drink, which has won many international awards, is a blend of cream and Irish whiskey.

Niche Drinks, run by locals Ciaran Mulgrew (right), Michael Corry and Robin Young, now intend to open a new £15 million distillery on the outskirts of Derry, where they will distil Irish whiskey. The company will expand their 90-strong workforce as part of the development, and they are tipped to name their new blend after Amelia Earhart, the American aviation pioneer who landed in Derry after her first solo flight across the Atlantic in 1932.

Left: Amelia Earhart, pictured on the outskirts of Derry after her pioneering solo flight across the Atlantic.

Below: Niche Drinks, the current home of St Brendan's Irish Cream Liqueur in the Waterside area of the city.

Broighter Gold

In 1896, Tom Nicholl, a ploughman in the townland of Broighter, just outside Limavady, County Derry, unearthed a hoard of gold artefacts dating from the Iron Age (1st century BC). The Broighter Hoard, which is now on display in the National Museum of Ireland, has been described as the 'finest example of La Tene gold-working in Europe'.

The area where the discovery was made is now used to grow rapeseed, used in the production of rapeseed oil by Leona and Richard Kane.

Broglasco Farm in Myroe is located on the edge of Lough Foyle just above sea level on reclaimed land. The fertile ground grows high-yielding crops of wheat, barley, oilseed and potatoes. The Kanes have been

farming in this area for well over 100 years. Richard, a fourth generation farmer, now works the land with the latest machinery using traditional methods, with modern techniques.

The Kanes are always looking to diversify and one of their recent products now receives national and international recognition ie Broighter Gold Rapeseed Oil which is their premium cooking oil brand.

The award-winning Broighter Gold has tangible health benefits and is one of the best oils you can buy due to its balance of fatty acids. It is high in monounsaturated and polyunsaturated fats such as Omega 3, 6 and 9, that can help to lower cholesterol and it contains a lower level of saturated fatty acids compared to other vegetable oils.

Rapeseed oil also has a higher boiling/ smoking temperature leaving the goodness of the oil in the meal.

I have found Broighter Gold Rapeseed Oil to be the ideal culinary oil as it can be used in a variety of ways including frying, baking, roasting and is ideal for delicately flavoured dishes and salads.

Leona Kane of
Broighter Gold.

The Slow Food Co: Traditional Artisan Breads

After several years of dreaming, planning and building, artisan baker Kemal Scarpello of the Slow Food Co opened Ireland's first fully functional wood-fired brick oven bakery in County Donegal in 2013.

In keeping with the Slow Food Co ethos they have followed classic, centuries-old wood-fired methods to bring real bread back to life. Their craft breads range from rustic country whites and overnight sourdoughs to traditional Irish wheaten and sodas, French-style baguettes, spelt loaves, and gluten-free products. All are healthy, local and fresh.

Their aim is to reintroduce an understanding of the importance of pure, freshly baked breads, and in doing so try to satisfy modern demand for authentic, carefully made products, far removed from the mechanisation and mass production of today's baking industry, where additives, improvers and preservatives are standard.

Their breads have few ingredients, the best available and as local as possible:

Stone-ground organic flour from the UK, sea salt and water from Ireland. Free range eggs, milk and butter come from local producers and when in season, fruit and vegetables are picked on the day from their own walled garden and poly-tunnel.

All their loaves are hand formed, risen for long periods to develop flavour, and baked to wood-fired perfection in a stone oven. Many of the breads are made using only natural yeast which is harnessed over time using just organic flour and natural mineral water which enhances further the complex flavour of their breads. They produce only small quantities, some 100 loaves a day, which they supply to local shops, restaurants and farmers' markets. Home delivery is also available by advance notice. Visit www.slowfood-co.com for more info on Slow Food Co.

Brian McDermott: The No-Salt Chef

Inishowen man Brian McDermott is one of only a handful of Irish chefs with a Culinary Arts Degree, graduating top of his class. A successful career working in the kitchens of some of his native Donegal's most-lauded establishments, and a senior global product development role in Kerry Group, ended for health reasons. As a result, Brian changed his lifestyle, and consequently his cooking style, and quickly established a reputation for himself as 'The No-Salt Chef', cooking great tasting, accessible and affordable food without adding salt. Brian has his own weekly cookery slot on BBC Radio Foyle and is a regular contributor to many Irish press titles.

The Brian McDermott Cookery School is also providing a unique 'Chef's Table' experience catering for groups of up to 14 people with a very personal culinary journey comprising a seven-course tasting menu. Guests are greeted with a complimentary drink and canapés and then get to dine with Brian who will cook each course, explaining the dish and using the best of local produce. The Chef's Table experience is already becoming very popular for family gatherings, fun nights out and celebrating special occasions.

Aiming to attract participants from across Ireland, North and South, Brian has partnered with the nearby four-star Redcastle Oceanfront Golf and Spa Hotel for accommodation for the school.

My own modest contribution to Derry's reputation as a culinary centre, I hope, has been the establishment of the Irish Food Heritage Project (IFHP), which aims to revisit, explore and celebrate the island's culinary legacy – and revive the traditional Irish rural way of life. This entails organising showcase demonstrations, tours, education and outreach events, and engaging the community through publications like this one and the accompanying digital app.

One practical example of the IFHP's early success has been our support for the campaign to re-introduce the lumper potato into Ireland. Already, 12 Derry schools are taking part in a unique project to grow the potato, which has effectively been extinct since the Great Famine. The scheme is led by Michael McKillop of **Glens of Antrim Potatoes**, and Gareth Austin, local horticulturist, and encourages young people to take an interest in agriculture, food and history.

Above: The Irish Food Heritage Project is proud to support, and work with, a wide range of food producers and suppliers across the North West and beyond.

Right: Emmett McCourt, Director of the Irish Food Heritage Project, winner at the NI Food and Drink Awards 2013.

Below: The Project was also nominated at the 2013 Licensed and Catering News Awards sponsored by Diageo.

The response across the island to our IFHP initiatives has been very positive. People have never been as aware of the importance of local produce, and they are becoming genuinely excited about the benefits of sourcing and growing their own food wherever they can and cooking it in the most healthy way possible. Indeed, given our magnificent history and the huge passion people of all ages and means are now demonstrating in their food heritage, I would say there has never been a better time to be involved in the food business in Ireland. So pull up a chair to the table and enjoy.

Happy eating, *ithe sásta* and *bon appétit*!

All over the North West of Ireland you will find amazing colourful characters working the land, cultivating crops and tending livestock. Their vast knowledge and expertise gained over a lifetime of hard labour and training in traditional Irish farming ways are gradually dying out. You can see the wit, wisdom and weather in the faces of these country folk, captured by photographer Sue Spencer in rural Donegal.

I am a great advocate of using fresh, natural, locally sourced ingredients. You would be amazed how many varieties of wild mushroom you can forage for in your local forest. However, not all are suitable or safe for eating so expert guidance is essential. If there are any specialist tours in your area, they will guide you to the correct locations and indicate the types of fungi to look for. The difference in taste and flavour these wild mushrooms produce is amazing. I use them in a range of my signature dishes.

Inishowen Bog Oak

A few years ago I came across Mary Doherty's wonderful workshop in Bocan, just outside Culdaff, where she has created a gallery of unique sculptures crafted from 6,000-year-old Irish bogwood.

Our ancestors used bog fir and bog oak for the couples and ribs of their houses. The bark from bog oak was also used for making the attachments in beds under the chaff and straw mattresses. 'Creepies' can still be found in old Irish homes (small stools made from bogwood and fireside chairs hewn from bog oak).

Mary has exhibited her sculptures nationally and internationally to much acclaim, and her work has been highly sought after by customers across Europe and the United States.

Mary's enthusiasm for her craft is infectious: once the bog oak has been unearthed it is left to dry naturally and the long and arduous task of bringing the piece to life then begins. Each piece is sculpted, carefully sanded and then coated in beeswax to give it a natural sheen that needs no further polishing.

I have commissioned several pieces of unique 6,000 year-old bog oak sculptures which I use as traditional serving plates and display platters for some of my signature heritage dishes. I highly recommend a visit to her workshop if you want an original souvenir piece of unique Irish tradecraft.

The Irish Food Heritage Project has been busy all over the country and I have had the great pleasure of working and engaging with a range of wonderfully talented and charismatic individuals and organisations at a variety of culinary/cultural events and game fairs in recent years. These are just some of these great memories.

The Irish Food Heritage Project was retained to provide a range of traditional seafood dishes using fresh Lough Foyle native flat oysters and a live culinary demonstration to advertise the launch of the Turner Prize during the City of Culture celebrations in Derry in 2013.

The Haven Smokehouse:
Irish Turf-Smoked Salmon

Sue Cruse and Declan McConnellogue are firm believers in tradition. They contest that the old ways are the best, and to that end they built a traditional timber-framed smokehouse on their land in Carrigart in Donegal.

They source their salmon from Fanad, fresh and out of the sea for no more than a few hours before being placed in the smokehouse. The fish are filleted and prepared for smoking, with no mechanical interference. The salmon are hung on hooks and smoked using turf and beechwood for a few days. The fish are in high demand from many of the best restaurants in Donegal and further afield and the Haven Smokehouse is making a great name for itself in culinary circles as an artisan quality traditional heritage seafood specialist. Small indigenous artisan food producers like Haven Smokehouse are what this project is all about – they embody the spirit and ethos of the Irish Food Heritage Project and we wish them every success in the future.

Above: Although the Irish Food Heritage Project's main focus is the preservation and culinary revival of traditional Irish food, we are avid connoisseurs of international cuisine. We are fascinated to see how multi-ethnic dishes and ingredients have influenced modern interpretations of traditional Irish dishes, particularly the addition of spices and exotic vegetables. Essentially, the base ingredient of the majority of our traditional dishes is the potato. But it is fascinating to see how these dishes are transformed by the simple substitution of another staple like pasta or rice.

Below: Dorothy Ryan, proprietor of Donegal Prime Fish, with Paul Murray inspecting the lobster catch. Also company founder Reggie Ryan (below centre) with record halibut catch. Donegal Prime Fish source the finest produce for my signature seafood dishes.

Right: Emma Cowan of *Flavour* Magazine with master rabbit warrener/ expert Steven McGonigal, pictured below right, with a catch of bucks, perfect for my saddle of Inishowen rabbit.

Above: Jamesy Quinn and Phil Cunningham, wildlife enthusiasts, anglers and Derry gentleman, fishing on the Faughan in 2010.

Below: Celebrity chefs Nick Nairn and Paul Rankin filming for *Paul and Nick's Big Food Trip* on the Foyle Marina in 2012. (Courtesy of Waddle Media.)

The Irish Food Heritage Project captured at a range of events over the last few years. These include: (above right) the staff and students of the North West Regional College at Worldskills, 2012 (Birmingham NEC); (above and opposite) a cookery demonstration at Richmond Hall, Foyle Parents and Friends Association (courtesy Peter McKane); (below) Ballymagroarty Community Group Allotment Project. Many of my food demonstrations have been kindly supported by Flogas and I find there is no reliable alternative to using gas-powered hobs for the level of temperature control and instant heat that they provide.

Recipes from Contributing Chefs/Cooks

The following recipes were very kindly contributed by several good friends who were more than happy to support the Irish Food Heritage Project. The recipes reflect their own food tastes and culinary heritage and how that heritage has travelled to the New World and impacted on other nations.

CHAPTER 20

Passing on the Poundies

Noel McMeel

Noel is Executive Head Chef of the Lough Erne Resort in Enniskillen, County Fermanagh, where he cooked for world leaders at the G8 summit in 2013. He was awarded Ulster Chef of the Year by The Restaurants Association of Ireland in 2011. Noel is a passionate ambassador for local produce and I had the great pleasure of training under him at the Beechill Country House Hotel in Ardmore, County Derry. He was previously Executive Chef at Castle Leslie in County Monaghan where he cooked and prepared the food for former Beatle Paul McCartney's wedding to Heather Mills in 2002.

Noel wrote to me to contribute his recipes to the project:

These are two recipes that were always made at home on special occasions. Almost everyone around Toomebridge and the fishermen of Lough Neagh celebrated Halloween with eel suppers. Boxty was always a border thing made by potatoes, flour and some butter and pan-fried. If you poached them they were known as 'hurlies'.

Smoked Eel Mousse with Boxty Pancakes, Horseradish and Mustard Grain Cream and Fresh Herb Salad

Ingredients (Serves 4)

500g raw fresh eel fillets, skinned
1 medium egg white
olive oil
125ml chilled double cream
250g smoked eel fillets (Lough Neagh)
diced small handful each of fresh coriander, basil, chervil, and rocket leaves
salt and pepper

Boxty Pancakes

125g raw peeled potato (a floury variety such as Dunbar Standard or Maris Piper)
125g mashed potato, made from 200g floury potatoes, peeled and cooked
125g plain flour, plus extra for dusting, ½ tsp baking powder, ½ tsp salt, large knob of salted butter, melted and cooled, some milk if needed.

Horseradish and Mustard Grain Cream

300ml whipping cream
1 tsp freshly grated horseradish
1 tsp wholegrain mustard, preferably Castle Leslie

Method

1. Make the smoked eel mousse. Check the fresh eel for any stray bones or skin, then work the flesh to a fine purée in a blender. Add the egg white and a pinch of salt, purée again, then press the mixture through a very fine sieve into a bowl, checking again that there are no bones. Place the bowl over a bowl of ice and chill in the fridge for 10-15 minutes.

2. Preheat the oven to 150C/Gas 2. Lightly brush four 7.5-10cm non-stick moulds

with olive oil. (Or use oiled ramekins lined with discs of non-stick baking parchment.)

3. Remove the purée from the fridge and mix in the cream with a rubber spatula. Do this very slowly or the mixture may curdle. Fold in the smoked eel, season, and spoon into the moulds. Cover the moulds and stand them in a roasting tin, then pour in enough warm water to come halfway up their sides. Bake *au bain marie* for 8 minutes, or until a knife inserted in the centre comes out clean. Remove from oven and leave to cool.

4. Make the boxty pancakes. Grate the raw potato into a bowl. Turn out onto a cloth and wring over a bowl, catching the liquid. This will separate into a clear fluid with starch at the bottom. Pour off and discard the fluid, then scrape out the starch and mix it with the grated and mashed potatoes. Sift the dry ingredients and mix into the potatoes with the melted butter, adding a little milk if necessary to make a pliable dough. Knead lightly on a floured surface. Divide into four and form flat round cakes that are about 1cm larger than the moulds used for the eel mousse. With the back of a knife, mark each pancake into quarters without cutting right through.

5. Heat a large griddle or heavy frying pan until hot. Dust with flour, then place a pancake marked-side down on the pan. Cook over a medium heat for 3-5 minutes until browned. Turn the pancake over and repeat on the other side.

6. Meanwhile, make the horseradish cream. Whip the cream until it holds a peak, then fold in the horseradish, mustard, and salt and pepper to taste. Mix the salad leaves together and season with sea salt and small drop of olive oil.

7. To serve, put a pancake, marked-side up, on each plate, and un-mould an eel mousse onto it. Serve immediately, garnished with salad and quenelles of horseradish cream.

Seasonal Berry Custards with a Baked Oat Crumble and Lavender Honey Ice Cream

Ingredients (Serves 4)

9 medium egg yolks
250g caster sugar
1 vanilla pod, split lengthways
1 litre whipping cream
200g mixed seasonal berries
juice of ½ lemon
100ml lavender honey

Crumble

100g plain flour
50g porridge oats
70g salted butter
50g caster sugar

Method

1. Put the egg yolks and 200g of the caster sugar in a bowl. Scrape the vanilla seeds from the pod, add to the bowl, and mix together by hand with a whisk. Bring the cream and the vanilla pod to the boil, add to the egg mixture and mix thoroughly. Divide the custard into two halves, discarding the pieces of vanilla pod. Cool one half rapidly over a bowl of ice and chill in the fridge for 10-15 minutes.

2. Preheat the oven to 170C/Gas 3.

3. Place the berries in a saucepan with the remaining caster sugar and the lemon juice. Poach gently for 3-4 minutes, then place the berries in the bottom of four 12cm

moulds or cups, and pour the unchilled custard on top. Place in a roasting tin, pour in warm water to come halfway up the sides of the moulds, then bake *au bain marie* for 30 minutes or until the custards are just set – they should wobble like a jelly when tapped. Remove from the oven, leave to cool, then put in the fridge. Keep the oven on.

4. Make the crumble. Put all the ingredients into a food processor and blitz quickly.

Spread out on a baking sheet and bake at the same temperature as the custards for 10-15 minutes until golden. Leave to cool.

5. Make the ice cream. Mix the chilled custard and lavender honey together, churn in an ice-cream machine until thickened, or just put it into the freezer and whisk every 30 minutes for 1½ hours then put it into a new container and freeze.

6. To serve, top the chilled berry custards with the crumble and ice cream.

Judith McLoughlin

I met Judith in 2013 when she brought her Shamrock & Peach Food Tours to Ireland. Judith linked up with me in the new Feast or Famine Food Adventures of Derry which were well received by her American visitors. Judith has kindly shared with us a few recipes from her very successful cook book *The Shamrock and Peach* with fantastic photos from her husband Gary.

Judith Johnson McLoughlin is an Irish cook with a passion for good food and the art of great hospitality. Originally from County Armagh in the heart of rural Northern Ireland, she learned the techniques of the Scots-Irish culinary tradition from her family who had generations of experience in the Irish hospitality and restaurant business before deciding on a move to the United States with her husband Gary. After spending a short time in the Boston area, they settled in Roswell, Georgia, just outside Atlanta, where Judith started her own gourmet food business called 'The Ulster Kitchen'. Specialising in Scots-Irish cuisine, Judith has created her own unique food fusion by blending the techniques of her homeland with the new-found flavours of the South to great acclaim. Judith teaches Irish cooking at many venues and has made numerous television and media appearances and is busy throughout the year

cooking and catering in Atlanta and beyond.

Judith's husband, Gary McLoughlin, is an artist, designer and photographer with many years of experience in professional design, layout and composition. Gary also grew up in County Armagh in Northern Ireland but now resides in Atlanta with Judith and their two boys, Peter and Jack. He has a love for the Irish landscape in photography and is currently pursuing a new project entitled 'The Irish Image' to showcase the wild beauty that is Ireland. You can find further examples of his work at: www.theirishimage.com

Fig and Fennel Skillet Cornbread with Irish Cheddar Cheese

Creek Native Americans in Tennessee and Georgia were using corn in all sorts of ways for generations before European settlers arrived, and, given its versatility, it's no wonder the new arrivals picked up on this staple and blended it with their homeland techniques. The simple list of ingredients found in this famous Southern quick-bread resembles Irish soda or wheaten, and I cannot help but imagine how the Scots-Irish settlers improvised and adapted to the newfound colourful cornmeal. I love the crunchy outside contrasted with the soft cake-like consistency of this bread, while the fennel seeds provide an interesting liquorish flavour that blends perfectly with the sweet figs and salty cheese.

Ingredients (Serves 4-6)

2 tbsp melted butter (or bacon fat)
6 oz (1½ cups) all-purpose flour (sifted)
4 oz (1 cup) stone-ground cornmeal
2 tbsp sugar
2 tsp baking powder (sifted)
½ tsp salt
4 oz (1 cup) aged Irish cheddar cheese (grated)
8 fl oz (1 cup) buttermilk
4 tbsp vegetable oil (you can substitute melted butter)
1 egg (beaten)
5 figs (cut into eighths)
1 tbsp fennel seeds

Method

1. Preheat the oven to 400F/Gas 6.
2. Grease a small 8-inch cast-iron skillet or baking pan with butter.
3. Place the skillet into the oven to preheat.
4. Combine the flour, cornmeal, sugar, salt, and baking powder in mixing bowl. Stir in the cheese and fennel seeds.
5. In another bowl, whisk together the egg, buttermilk and vegetable oil. Combine the wet and dry ingredients together and stir with a large metal spoon to mix.
6. Remove the preheated skillet from the oven and pour in the batter.
7. Press the figs into batter and arrange in a circular fashion.
8. Bake the cornbread for 25 minutes.
9. Remove from the oven and set skillet on a rack to cool for 10 minutes before slicing and serving.

Coke-Soaked Braised Venison
with Creamy Potato and Parsnip Mash

We have a generous Southern friend who enjoys sport shooting and supplies us with venison during the hunting season in Georgia. He was also generous enough with us to share his unique marinade for venison using Coca-Cola to tenderize the meat. To an Irish immigrant such as I, this was such an unusual meal concept but one which tasted surprisingly delicious, and I just had to include it in my 'Coming to America' chapter in *The Shamrock and Peach*. I am sure those early Scots-Irish immigrants also had their fair share of deer hunting as they settled the Appalachians. Enjoy!

Ingredients (Serves 4)

Coke Marinade
2 fl oz (¼ cup) coke
2 tbsp vegetable oil
1 tbsp soy sauce
1 tbsp Worcester sauce
1 garlic clove (crushed)
¼ tsp freshly milled black pepper
¼ tsp kosher salt

Venison Stew
3 slices of thick cut bacon
1 tbsp olive oil
2lbs venison back strap (cut into 2-ins strips)
4 tbsp all purpose flour
½ tsp kosher salt
¼ tsp pepper
3 medium onions (peeled and thickly sliced)
4 carrots (peeled and cut into 1-ins strips)
12 fl oz (1½ cups) red wine
1 pint (2 cups) beef stock
2 tbsp red currant jelly
2 tbsp tomato purée
sprig of thyme (1 tsp chopped)
2 bay leaves

Parsnip and Potato Mash
5 medium-sized potatoes (cut into 1-inch pieces)
3 medium-sized parsnips (scraped and cut into 1-inch pieces)
2 oz (¼ cup) melted butter
6 tbsp heavy whipping cream
½ tsp salt
¼ tsp white pepper
pinch of grated fresh nutmeg

Method
For the Marinade and Venison
1. Combine the ingredients for marinade together and soak the venison in this marinade overnight in a zip-lock bag.
2. In a large skillet, cook the bacon until crisp then remove from pan.
3. Remove meat from marinade and drain.
4. Toss the marinated venison meat in flour seasoned with salt and pepper.
5. Preheat oven to 350F/Gas 4.
6. Drain off a little bacon grease, reserving 2 tbsp for sautéing.
7. Heat the remaining fat to medium-hot and add the meat to the skillet in small batches, searing for 2-3 minutes on each side.
8. Transfer to a Dutch-style oven or deep casserole dish with a lid.
9. Add a little oil to the skillet and sauté the onions until soft before adding carrots and cook for 2 more minutes.
10. Transfer the vegetables to the dish with the seared meat.
11. Deglaze the skillet with the red wine. Add the stock, thyme, bay leaves, tomato purée, and red currant jelly, stirring to combine.
12. Pour the resulting liquid over the meat and vegetables, place in the oven, and bake for 1 hour.

13. Add bacon and cook for 15 more minutes, then remove the bay leaves and discard.

14. To serve, place a large spoonful of parsnip and potato mash in centre of the plate, making a well. Spoon the venison stew into the potato parsnip nest and garnish.

For the Potato and Parsnip Mash
1. Place the potatoes and parsnips into a medium saucepan with enough cold water to cover the vegetables.

2. Bring to a boil and cook for 15 minutes until soft.

3. Drain vegetables then run through a potato ricer before mashing with butter, cream, salt, pepper, and nutmeg.

Ford's Southern Farmstead Fried Chicken

My friend Ford Fry is an extraordinary chef who has a flair for making the most wonderful Southern food. He has taken the farmstead style of cooking to a new level in Atlanta and has graciously shared with me his famous JCT Southern Fried Chicken recipe. This delicious and wonderfully moist fried chicken takes a little planning and time to prepare, but it's worth it to get a dish that will have your guests sucking on the bones and licking their fingers to no end! Not strictly a 'grill dish', I know, but fried chicken is a wonderful Southern cookout tradition.

Ingredients (Makes 16 pieces)

Southern Fried Chicken
2 whole organic 3-3½lbs chicken (each cut into 8 pieces)

For the Brine
8 pints (1 gallon) water
8 oz (1 cup) kosher salt
2 oz (¼ cup) sugar
1 bay leaf
1 tbsp black peppercorns
1 bunch of fresh thyme

Second Soak
1½ pints (3 cups) buttermilk

For the Seasoned Flour
16 oz (4 cups) flour
4 oz (1 cup) cornstarch
2 tbsp kosher salt
2 tbsp black pepper
2 tbsp granulated garlic
1 tbsp cayenne pepper
2 tsp ground nutmeg

For the Fry
canola oil for frying

Method
Day one:
1. Using an appropriate sized pot, place all 6 ingredients of the brine together and bring to a boil.

2. Turn off the heat and let the liquid cool to room temperature.

3. Place the chicken pieces into a large sealable bowl or container, completely cover with the room temperature brine, and place in the refrigerator for 24 hours.

Day two:
1. Once the chicken has brined, strain off all the brine liquid and discard the herbs.

2. Cover chicken with buttermilk and return to the refrigerator until you are ready to fry.

Frying:

1. Using a large cast-iron skillet and a deep-fat thermometer, fill the skillet halfway with canola oil then heat the oil to 300F/Gas 2. (The oil temperature should fluctuate between 280-300F.)

2. Once oil is stable, drain off the buttermilk from the bowl and dredge the chicken pieces into the seasoned flour. Pat off any excess and carefully place into the hot oil. Repeat with all the remaining chicken pieces.

3. Once the chicken becomes golden brown on one side (roughly 10 minutes), turn over and brown on the other side. (To be safe, place a meat thermometer into the chicken closest to the centre and next to the bone. The temperature should read no less than 160F/73C.)

4. Remove the chicken from the oil and rest the pieces on a rack-lined tray, allowing them to drain.

5. If you will be making chicken in batches, feel free to hold the completed chicken pieces in a 200F oven until you are ready to serve.

6. Sprinkle with herbs and serve right away.

Mary M Drymon

The three recipes Mary Drymon has kindly shared with us are from her publication *Scotch-Irish Foodways In America* which contains a wide range of recipes obtained from historic sources and cookbooks, and carefully treasured variations gathered from food historians, family members, and friends. They are by no means to be considered the final word but rather a basis that can be added to in the future.

Mary Drymon was trained in the art of open-hearth cooking at the Israel Crane House in Montclair, New Jersey, and took classes at Colonial Williamsburg in Virginia. She learned how to cook on a woodstove in her grandmother's kitchen. She had a lengthy career as a museum curator, developing recipes and curricula for historic cooking classes for both adults and children that were conducted in working museum kitchens.

Mary has cooked these recipes using an open hearth and woodstove cooking techniques as well as on a modern stove. Many work in each format, although the modern stove does not impart the same taste of history to foodstuffs as the slow, sometimes smoky process of earlier cooking methods. The ingredients in the recipes can be either grown at home or can, in most cases, be found locally The recipes are traditional and usually pre-date 1900.

As Mary herself comments:

> While the Scotch-Irish have all too often been interpreted by others, to themselves, traditional foodways have been a way of life. In a log cabin home, when work was done for the day, supper cooked, eaten and cleared away, and the fiddles and pipes were brought out, it was time for the fireside ceilidhs that animated the American back country and tied them through Ulster back to their Scottish homeland. After harvesting the fruits of a year's worth of hard work in the fields, the Scotch-Irish up and down the Appalachian Mountains would celebrate by joining together with neighbours and family, dancing, and singing. These celebrations would usually include harvest tables laden with traditional foods and spirits, cooked simply using well water and local ingredients over an open-hearth fire or a woodstove. And, speaking with those who grew up eating food cooked in such a way, there is no better meal available than one cooked in such conditions.

From *Scotch-Irish Foodways In America: Recipes From History* by MM Drymon. *The 1718 Project: Celebrating 300 Years of Ulster Scot Culture in America, 1718-2018.*

Hoe (or Johnny) Cakes

The term 'hoe cake' comes from the method once used to bake them on the iron blade of a hoe in a fireplace or over an open fire. The term 'Johnny cakes' may be a corruption of journey cakes in that they kept well while travelling.

Traditional Recipe

Scald 1 pint of milk and put to 3 pints of Indian [corn] meal and half pint of flour. Bake before the fire. Or scald with milk two thirds of the Indian meal, or wet two thirds with boiling water, add salt, molasses and lard and work up with cold water to stiff, and bake as above.

Ingredients *for* Modern Recipe (Serves 8)
1 cup cornmeal
1 cup all-purpose flour
1 tsp baking powder
1 tsp baking soda
2 tbsp sugar
¼ cup bacon drippings
1 or 2 eggs
1 cup buttermilk

Method
1. Sift all the dry ingredients into a large mixing bowl.
2. Heat the bacon drippings in a heavy iron skillet. Pour off and reserve most of the grease but leave the skillet well oiled.
3. Add eggs and milk to the dry ingredients and mix until just blended. Add the hot bacon drippings and mix until well blended. Batter should be about the consistency of pancake batter, so you may need to add more buttermilk.
4. Cook the mixture. For hoe cake, cook over low flame on top of stove with skillet tightly covered for about 15 minutes. Flip and cook another 10 to 15 minutes on other side. To make Johnny cakes, pour the batter into the skillet and cook as you would pancakes.

Grits

The techniques of processing corn into grits represents knowledge imparted by the Cherokee to Scotch-Irish settlers in the Appalachian back country. A time-consuming process, it is somewhat more difficult than creating risotto.

Ingredients (Serves 4)
1 cup coarse grits
a quantity of spring water
sea salt
2 to 3 tbsp butter
½ tsp black pepper

Method
In a slow cooker:
1. Place the grits in the slow cooker and cover with 3 cups spring water. Stir once. Allow grits to settle a full minute, tilt the vessel, and skim off and discard the chaff and hulls from the top with a fine strainer.
2. Cover slow cooker and turn the heat setting to high. Cook, stirring once or twice, until the grits are creamy and tender mushy throughout and hold their shape on a spoon. This takes about two hours.
3. Season with 1 teaspoon sea salt to taste, black pepper and butter. Stir until butter melts.

In a saucepan:
1. Place grits in a medium heavy-bottomed saucepan and cover with 2½ cups spring water. Stir once. Allow the grits to settle a full minute, tilt the pan, and skim off the chaff and hulls with a fine strainer.
2. Cover and let soak overnight.
3. Set the saucepan over medium heat and bring to a simmer, stirring constantly with a wooden spoon, until the first starch takes hold, 5 to 8 minutes. Reduce the heat to the lowest possible setting and cover.
4. Meanwhile, heat 2 cups of water in a small saucepan and keep it hot. Cook the grits, covered, over low heat, stirring every 10 minutes or so, and adding small amounts of the hot water to the grits if they become too thick.
5. Cook until the grits are creamy and tender throughout, and hold their shape on a spoon. This will take between 1 and 1½ hours.
6. Add 1 teaspoon sea salt halfway through the cooking time. To finish, stir in the butter until melted. Add the black pepper and more salt to taste.

Rhubarb Custard

Rhubarb flourishes in the north of England and was brought over to America with Scotch-Irish settlers from the North West of Ireland. The use of orange juice in this custard offsets the natural tartness of the rhubarb, while the ginger adds a touch of spice.

Ingredients (Serves 4)
6 tbsp butter
¾ cup crushed Graham crackers
1lb fresh rhubarb stems, trimmed and cut into 1-inch lengths
3 tbsp water
finely grated rind and juice of 1 large orange
2 eggs, separated
¼ cup granulated sugar
2 tbsp cornstarch
½ tsp ground ginger

Method
1. Melt the butter in a saucepan, then mix in the Graham cracker crumbs.

2. Press the mixture over the base and sides of an 8-inch fluted pie dish or tin. Chill in the refrigerator while preparing the filling.

3. Put the rhubarb in a saucepan with water. Cover and simmer gently until the fruit is soft and pulpy. Stir occasionally to prevent the rhubarb sticking to the pan, purée with a handheld blender or in a food processor.

4. Put the orange rind and juice into a heavy-based saucepan. Add the egg yolks, sugar, cornstarch and ginger. Heat gently, stirring constantly, until thick. Stir into the rhubarb purée.

5. Whisk the egg whites until stiff. Fold gently into the rhubarb custard, then spoon the mixture into the Graham cracker crust. Refrigerate for at least 4 hours or overnight before serving.

Dr Áine Downey

Dr Áine Downey, a well-known and respected academic and Gaeilgeoir with roots in Donegal and Derry, generously provided this traditional Irish Apple Pie recipe made with potato bread pastry. She commented: 'Spud apple was usually made around Halloween in our house and it was a great treat for young and old alike.'

Spud Apple

Ingredients (Serves 4)
500g cooked, mashed potato (well drained)
500g plain flour
150g melted butter
salt and pepper to season
500g cooking apples, peeled, cored and chopped
2 tbsp lemon juice
100g sugar
25g butter
10g demerara

Method

1. Make your potato bread pastry as you would make it for an apple tart or apple pie for the oven. The better (and messier) way is the griddle.

2. Roll out to the size and thickness of 4 potato bread. Chop apples fairly small and stuff and fold the potato bread over as you would for a Cornish pasty.

3. Put a floured hot griddle on a fairly high heat.

4. When 'pastry' is starting to brown turn it over, usually three turnings.

5. About 20 minutes cooking time in total or cook in the oven at 180C/Gas 4.

6. Remove and smother all over in butter and demerara sugar. Be careful not to burn your tongue!!

Owensy's Creggan Poundies – Aka Champ

This recipe is kindly shared by my good friend, Creggan man and Master Chef Sean Owens, who sets the scene:

'My grandmother Cissie Murphy from Rinmore Drive in Derry's Creggan Estate was a great woman for whipping up the poundies (as were all the hard-pushed and hard-working women of Creggan). And if you were lucky, she would fry you a soft egg on top – simply heaven! Then my mother, Margaret Owens, would make the poundies on a Saturday with the massive pot bubbling away on the range cooker and the divine smell of the buttermilk and scallions and the fluffy potatoes dripping with freshly churned butter: a food memory that will last with me forever. Poundies is my soul food. This true classic Derry dish brings back a flood of memories of good times: safety, home, family, friends and loved ones. To all the great women of Creggan who brought up their weans on poundies – I salute you.'

Ingredients (Serves 4)
2kg peeled potatoes, cut down if too big
250ml (8 fl oz) milk
125ml buttermilk
10 scallions (spring onion), finely chopped
100g butter
salt and ground white pepper

Method
1. Place potatoes into large pot and cover with water.
2. Bring to the boil and cook until just 'to the bone' for about 20 minutes.
3. Teem the potatoes (ie remove the water by draining).
4. Put the drained potatoes back on the stove at a very low heat.
5. Let the potatoes dry out for a few minutes.
6. Put a clean dry tea towel over the potatoes to remove access moisture and set the pot to one side.
7. Heat the milk, buttermilk and scallions with half the butter gently in a new saucepan until warm.
8. Mash the potatoes, add salt and ground white pepper and the rest of the butter and beetle until smooth.
9. Stir in the milk and spring-onion mixture and beat.
10. Serve piping hot in a deep bowl with a knob of butter for each serving.

Variations: Nettle Poundies, Dulse Poundies, Burnt Onion Poundies. (For a real treat, top with two soft-poached free-range eggs or a couple of Paul Ellis's sausages.)

Further Reading

Physiologie du Gout: Jean Brillat Savarin. (Gabriel de Gonet Editeur, Paris, 1848)

Studies in Early Irish Law: DA Binchy et al. (Hodges Figgis, 1936)

The Brehon Laws, A legal Handbook: Laurence Ginnell. (TF Unwin, London, 1894)

Chronicles of Peru: Pedro de Cieza de León, Seville, 1553. (University of Pennsylvania Library, 2010)

An Historical Account of the Plantation in Ulster at the Commencement of the Seventeenth Century: George Hill. (McCaw, Stevenson & Orr, 1877)

A History Of Irish Cuisine: Before and After the Potato: John Linnane. (Dublin Institute of Technology, 2000)

The Potato in Irish Cuisine and Culture: Máirtín Mac Con Iomaire and Pádraic Óg Gallagher. (Dublin Institute of Technology, Articles, Paper 3, 2009)

The History and Influence of the Potato: Redcliffe Salaman. (Cambridge University Press, 1949)

A Little History of Irish Food: Regina Sexton. (Kyle Cathie Ltd, 1998)

A Short History of the Laggan Redshanks: 1569-1630: Barry R McCain. (Ulster Heritage, 2012)

Discover Derry: Brian Lacey. (Guildhall Press, 2011)

The Making of Derry: An Economic History: Brian Mitchell. (Genealogy Centre, 1992)

The History of Londonderry, comprising the towns of Derry and Londonderry NH: Rev Edward Lutwyche Parker. (Boston, Perkins and Whipple, 1851)

Georgian Cookery: Recipes and History: Jennifer Stead. (English Heritage, 2003)

Mrs Delany's Menus, Medicines and Manners: Katherine Cahill. (New Island, 2005)

1718 Migration: Scots Irish Journey to the New World: Dr James McConnel, Dr Linde Lunney, Dr William Roulston and Colin Brooks. (www.1718migration.org.uk)

The Ulster Scots and New England: Scotch-Irish Foundations in the New World: Alister McReynolds. (Ulster-Scots Community Network, 2010)

Along the Faughan Side: Olly McGilloway. (Dubh Regles Books, 1986)

Following the Foyle: A Portrait of the River Foyle: Ken McCormack and Pat Cowley. (Cottage Publications, 2008)

Samuel Gettys: The Adams County Historical Society: Joanne Lewis. (GCVB, 2012)

County Derry Roots of Jean Paul Getty: Brian Mitchell. (Genealogy Centre, 2011)

James Getty, The Siege of Derry and The Gettys of Ardnaguniog: Brian Mitchell and Bernadette Walsh. (Genealogy Centre, 2011)

Finding the McCains: Barry R McCain. (www.ulsterheritage.com)

History of the Port Of Derry (www.londonderryport.com)

Irish Corned Beef: A Culinary History: M Mac Con Iomaire and P Gallagher. (Journal of Culinary Science and Technology, Dublin Institute of Technology, 2011)

Scotch-Irish Foodways in America: Recipes from History: Mary M Drymon. (The 1718 Project, 2009)

Longest Running Court Battle on the River Foyle: Loughs Agency Archives. (*Derry Journal* 1947)

Donegal: The Making of a Northern County: Jim Mac Laughlin. (Four Courts Press, 2007)

Recipes For Peace: Over 100 Recipes to Promote Peace in Ireland: Marie Roche. (Vermilion, 1995)

A History of Irish Farming, 1750-1950: Jonathan Bell and Mervyn Watson. (Four Courts Press, 2008)

Ulster Farmers' Union: The History of its first Seventy Years 1917-1987: Alistair Mac Lurg. (Ulster Farmers' Union, 1989)

The Destructive Trade: Sean Beattie. (Donegal Annual, 1991)

The Book of Inistrahull: Sean Beattie. (Lighthouse Publications, 1997)

Donegal (Ireland in Old Photographs): Sean Beattie. (The History Press, 2004)

The Great Irish Famine: New Studies in Economic and Social History: Cormac Ó Gráda. (Cambridge University Press, 1995)

A Taste of Ireland: In Food and in Pictures: Theodora Fitzgibbon and George Morrison. (Pan Books, 1970)

Forgotten Skills of Cooking: The Time Honoured Ways are the Best: Darina Allen. (Kyle Cathie, 2009)

The Disappearing Irish Cottage: A case study of North Donegal: Clive Symmons and Seamus Harkin. (Wordwell Ltd, 2004)

The Popular Poets and Poetry of Ireland: Thomas C Irwin. (Richard Nagle, 1887)

Romantic Donegal: Its Songs, Poetry and Ballads: Harry Percival Swan. (Carter Publications, 1964)

Alexis Soyer: The First Celebrity Chef: Frank Clement-Lorford. (Amazon Kindle, 2011)

The Gastronomic Regenerator: a Simplified and Entirely New System of Cookery: Alexis Benoît Soyer. (Simpkin, Marshall & Co, London, 1847)

Bury My Heart at Wounded Knee: Dee Brown. (Holt, Rinehart and Winston of Canada Ltd, 1971)

Fair Day: Story of Irish Fairs and Markets: Patrick Logan. (Appletree Press, 1986)

The Book of Inishowen: Harry Percival Swan. (WM Doherty & Co, 1938)

Romantic Inishowen, Ireland's Wonderful Peninsula: Harry Percival Swan. (Hodges Figgis, 1948)

Hiring Fairs in Derry, Tyrone and Donegal: George Sweeney. (Guildhall Press, 1985)

Vanishing Ireland: Further Chronicles of a Disappearing World: James Fennell and Turtle Bunbury. (Hachette Books, 2009)

Italian Families in Derry: (*Derry Journal*, 2011)

Rick Stein's Seafood Lover's Guide: Rick Stein. (BBC Books, 2002)

Ireland: The Taste and the Country: Mick Bunn. (Anaya, 1994)

LegenDerry Food Guide: (Derry City Council, 2013)

The Shamrock and Peach: Judith McLoughlin. (Ambassador International, USA, 2011)

An Historical, Environmental and Cultural Atlas of County Donegal: Jim Mac Laughlin and Sean Beattie. (Cork University Press, 2013)

Index of Recipes